HOW TO DRAW HOUSES

By Sydney R. Jones

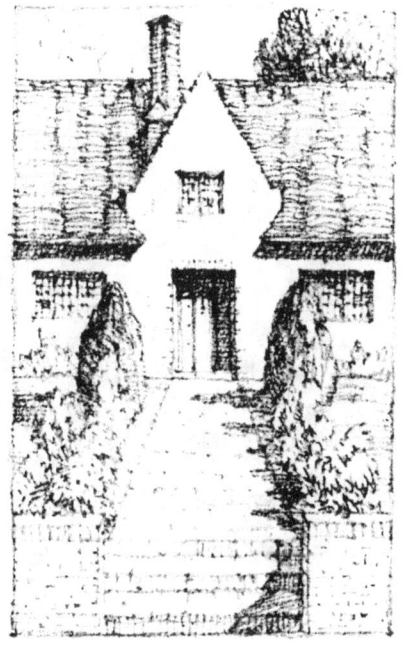

COACHWHIP PUBLICATIONS

Greenville, Ohio

How to Draw Houses, by Sydney R. Jones
Copyright © 2013 Coachwhip Publications
No claims made on public domain material.
First published 1946.
Front cover: House and landscape © Dmitry Rukhlenko

ISBN 1-61646-195-0
ISBN-13 978-1-61646-195-9

CoachwhipBooks.com

C O N T E N T S

HOUSE AND HOME

Everybody lives in a house of some kind. It may be a modern house or an old one, of big, small, or medium size, perhaps in a town, or maybe in the country. A large portion of our lives is spent inside and around them. At our houses, which become homes, we eat and sleep, enjoy family life, leisure, and the company of friends, go to a lot of trouble to make the rooms nice and comfortable, and if we want to sit quiet and read, have parties, listen to the wireless, or dabble in all sorts of private interests, there is " no place like home ". Our houses are our own particular quarters. They are the places in which we can live most freely. They become almost part of ourselves, for all homes, to a degree, reflect the character and ways of life of the people who reside in them.

Because house and home mean so much to the majority of people, it is not surprising that boys and girls, grown-ups, and quite young children also, often say, " I wish I could draw my house ". This is a very natural remark to make. But before the wish may end in good results, it is necessary to know how to proceed. John Ruskin once said, and with great truth, that almost anyone could learn to draw by really trying to do so. I therefore hope to shew the methods of drawing houses, in order that anyone who wishes to try may succeed in drawing his or her own house, and the homes of other people too.

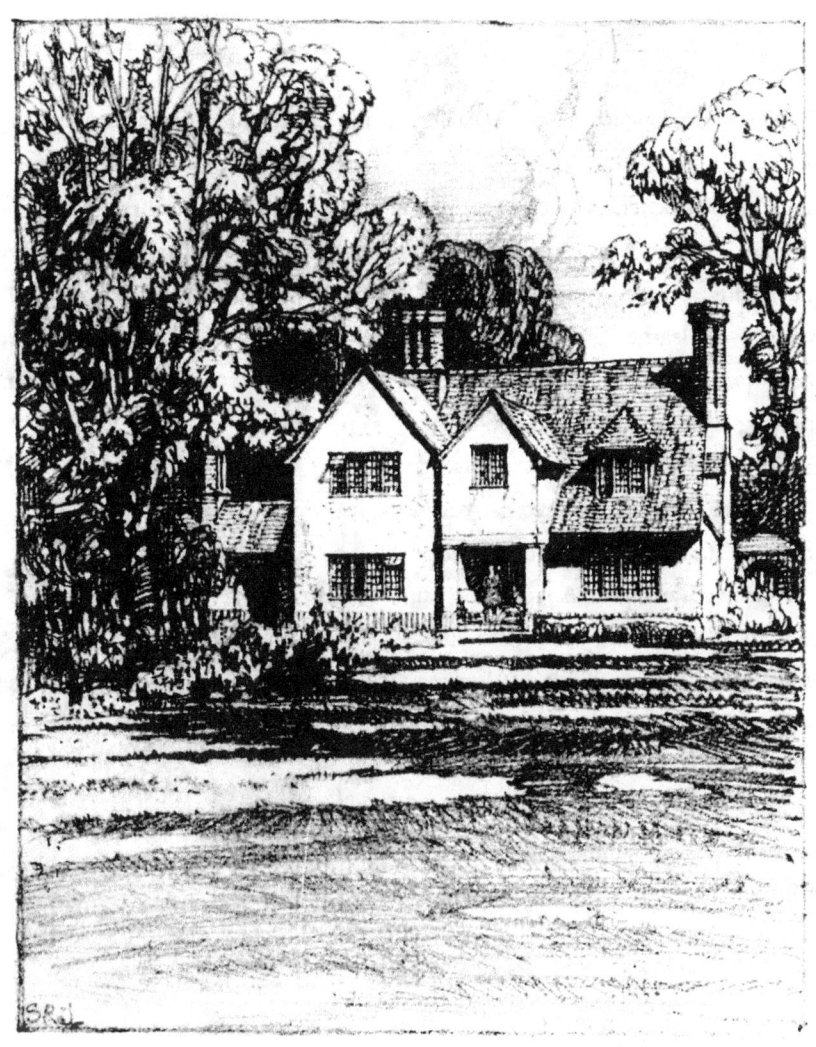

Pencil Drawing. A New House.

MATERIALS

Before commencing to work, materials for doing so of course have to be thought of. These are easily procured and need not cost much. Lead pencils black carbon pencils and crayons, pen and ink, and water colours, all may be used for drawing houses on paper. These materials play an important part in the results achieved. The particular effects that each material can give will have to be learned by constant practice. A pencil drawing, for example, looks quite different from one in pen and ink, and the character of a crayon,

drawing is unlike that of a water-colour. In the first instance, it is wise to master the uses of one material before thinking of others, and it is best to begin with pencil drawings. Anyone who can draw well in pencil will have little difficulty with other kinds of drawing.

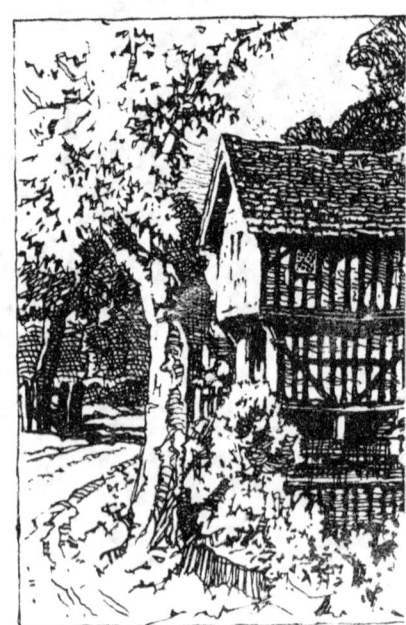

The paper for drawing may be of any kind, provided the pencil or other medium will work freely upon it. If the surface is not shiny, a pad of good writing paper is very suitable. Cartridge, hand-made, and other papers, can be obtained from shops for artists' materials. It is good to work on paper made up in pad or block form, for then each sheet keeps firm and smooth, and does not move while being used. If drawings are made on separate sheets of paper, each one must be fixed with drawing pins on to a card or drawing board.

Lead pencils vary from very hard to very soft. For first attempts the H.B. or B. is advisable ; in fact, the best way to gain skill is to try careful drawings with the H.B. pencil. When accomplishment has been gained, lovely effects are obtained with the 2, 3, and 4 B. grades. Sharpen the pencil very carefully by cutting the wood evenly all round, and leaving a point about half an inch long.

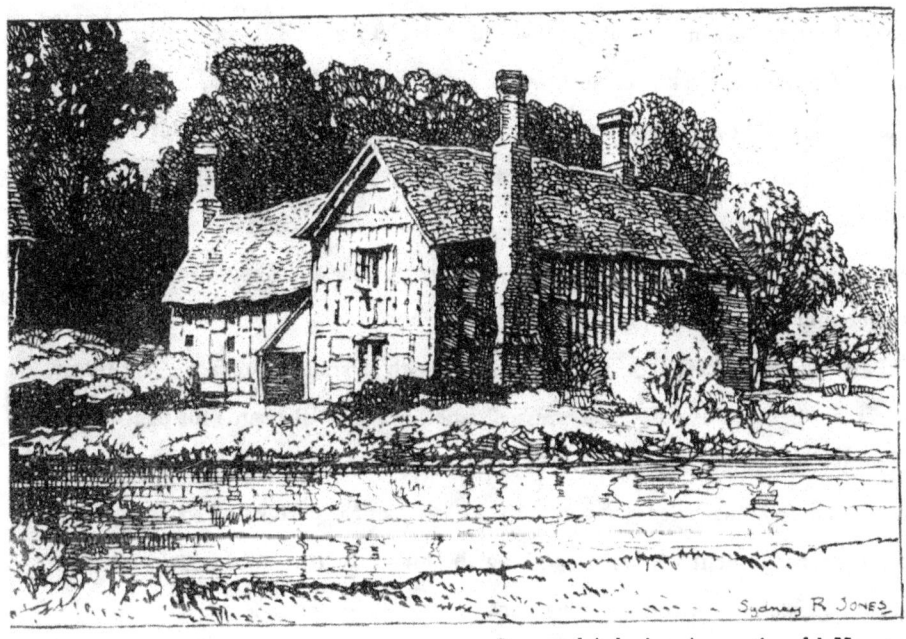

Pen and ink drawing. An old House.

9

A rubber is needed for removing mistakes. One end of it, cut to a point, will take out very small errors without disturbing the surrounding work. But if possible, it is best to acquire the way of drawing without making mistakes. One master who taught me did not allow rubbers. Of course neither I, nor my young companions, were clever enough to do without them, so we hid our rubbers in our pockets ! Through early training, however, I do not use a rubber much now.

Other kinds of pencils are made of carbon and conte crayon. The carbon ones are supplied in several grades, the H.B., B., and B.B. being the most useful for general work. Conte crayons are numbered 1, 2, and 3, No. 3 being the softest. They can give effects of much richness and beauty. But carbon and conte crayon pencils are only suitable when considerable skill in drawing has been acquired, for any mistakes made with them cannot be taken out easily. Crayons are brittle and very liable to break. They need care in sharpening with a keen knife or razor blade.

Pen drawings should be made on paper with a smooth surface. Writing paper can be most useful. Hot-pressed paper, and special boards for pen work also may be bought. Indian ink is sold in liquid form made up in bottles ; the indelible kind, called " fixed ", works well, and it permits of water-colour being washed over it without disturbing the line drawing. Writing pens with good, flexible points, and mapping pens for fine detail, complete the essentials for pen drawing.

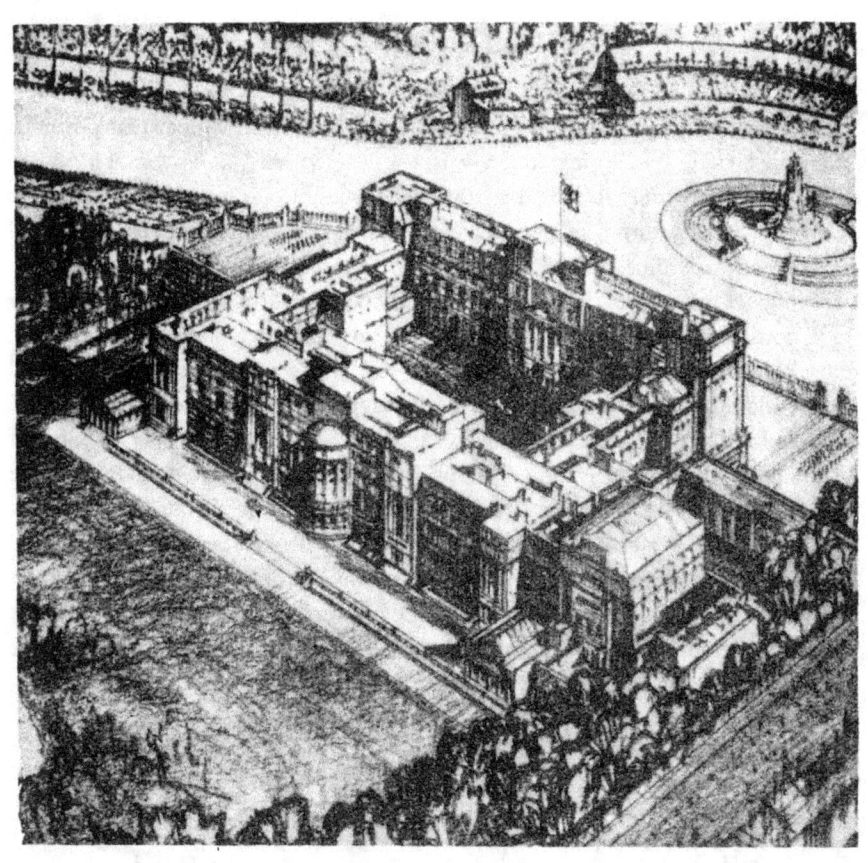

Crayon drawing. The Home of the King and Queen. Buckingham Palace.

FIRST THINGS FIRST

At the outset of experimenting on paper, it is well to remember that a famous man once said, " Learning to draw is learning to see ". To be able to see things properly only comes by training through practice. Study subjects carefully, noting form, shapes, structure, tones, and characteristics. Mental impressions are thus gained, and these are the foundations of expression in drawing. Quite a good idea is to thoroughly observe a subject—say the exterior of a house or the interior of a room—then go elsewhere, and try to draw all that has been seen and remembered. In this way a great deal can be learned by developing observation, memory and imagination.

Faced with the subject of a house, the first matter to decide is the point of view from which to draw it. This is important and needs thought, for the drawing will be disappointing if the point of view selected will not look well on paper, or makes a poor composition. Small trial sketches should be made from any angle of the building which offers possibilities. The one that shews the best grouping and effect will provide the basis for further work. Experience develops the ability to quickly select the good aspects of a subject, and to reject the unsatisfactory ones.

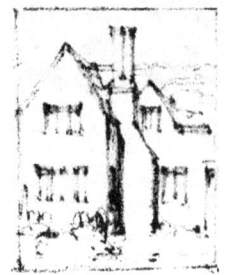 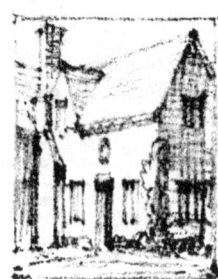 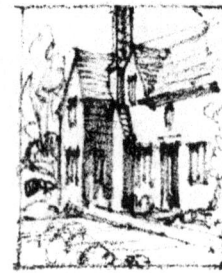

Trial sketches for selecting point of view.

12

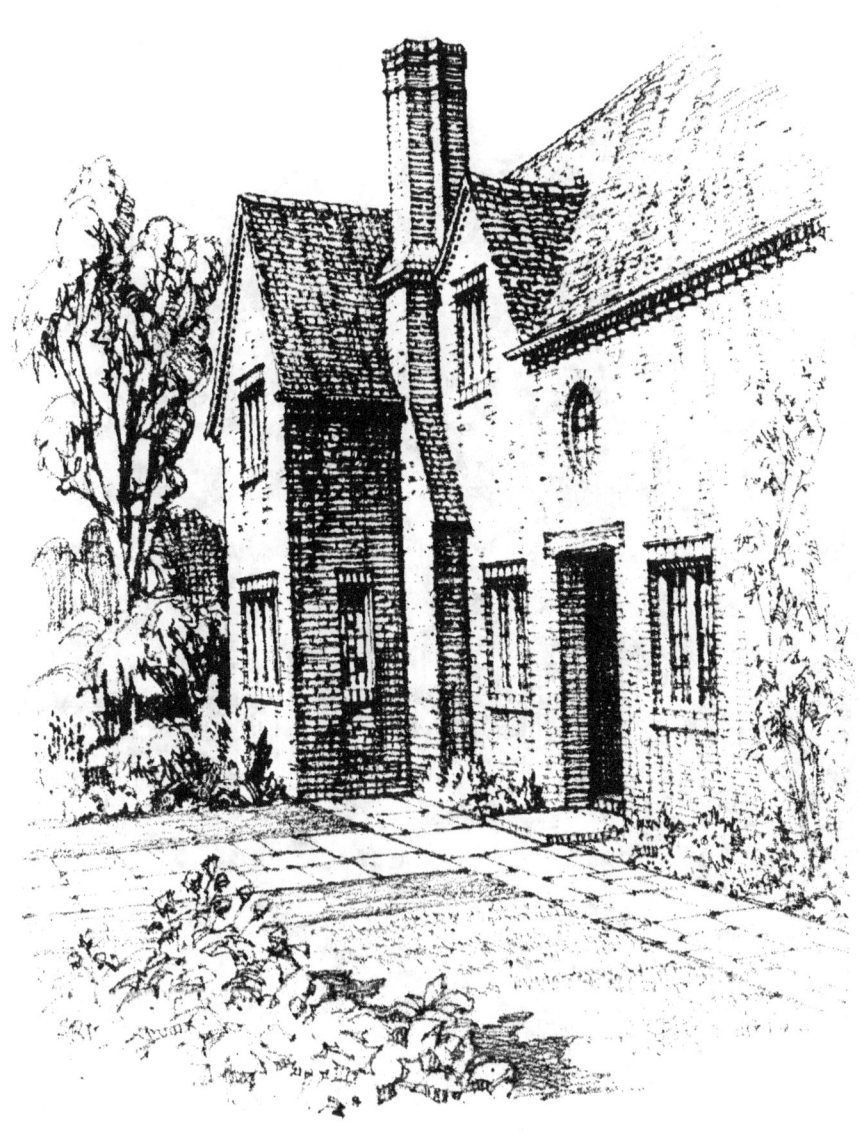

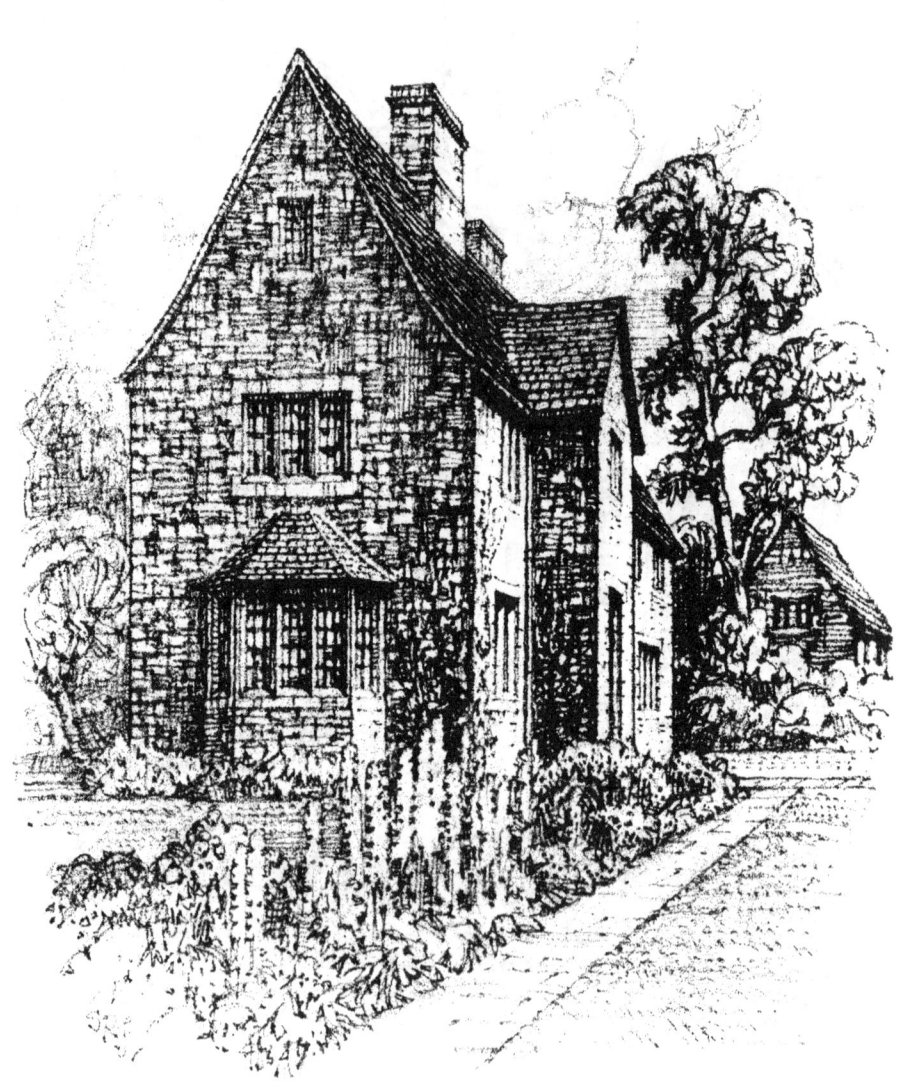

PLACING THE SUBJECT ON PAPER

Before commencing the real drawing, make sure that the view selected will come within the dimensions of the paper. This is done by first lightly indicating the main widths and heights. Although this advice may not seem necessary, even experienced draughtsmen sometimes find that the extent of the work has not been accurately judged, and they are short of the space to include the top, bottom, or sides of the picture.

Preliminary thought in this direction also ensures that the drawing will sit effectively within the limits of the space to be used, a further point of considerable consequence to the ultimate appearance of the work. Care thus taken with placing the subject rightly on the paper will prevent later disappointment, and the chance of having to start afresh.

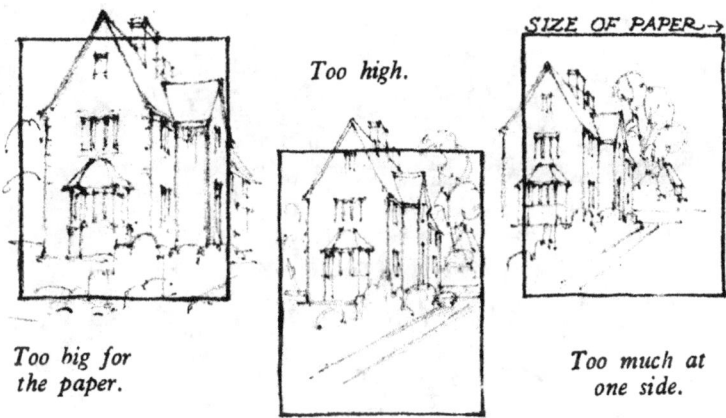

Too high.

SIZE OF PAPER →

Too big for the paper.

Too much at one side.

15

PROPORTION

An eye trained to gauge proportions is one of the elements for all good drawing. By gauging proportions, I mean the ability to determine, in terms of measurement, the relation of one part of the subject to another. In viewing a house, for example, the width of it may be seen to be twice as long as the height (figure 1); or the height of a doorway may be somewhat more than double the width, and also but one half of the height of the wall from the ground to the roof (figure 2). Similarly chimneys, windows (figure 3), and other features of houses, bear relation one to another in definite scales of proportion.

The relative sizes of shapes, both in the masses and in the details, must therefore be accurately seen and recorded if drawings of houses are to convey an idea of reality. This principle applies to drawing everything, and thus embraces the gardens, trees, and other surroundings of our homes.

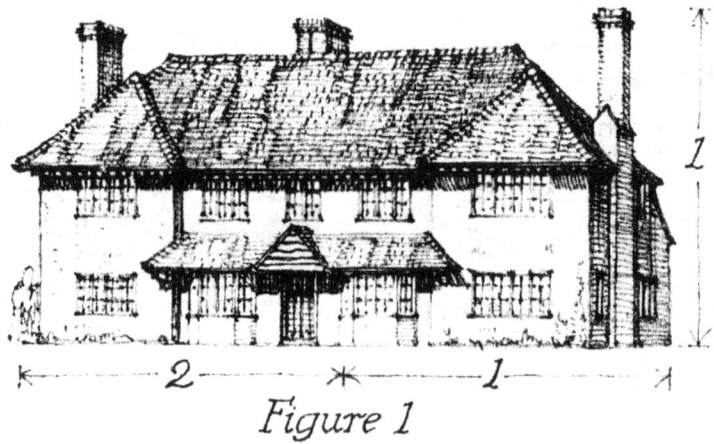

Figure 1

16

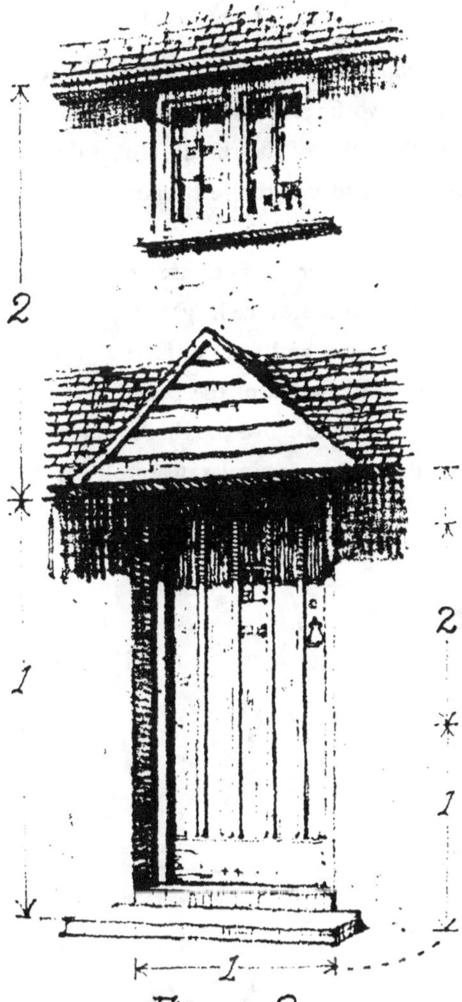

Figure 2

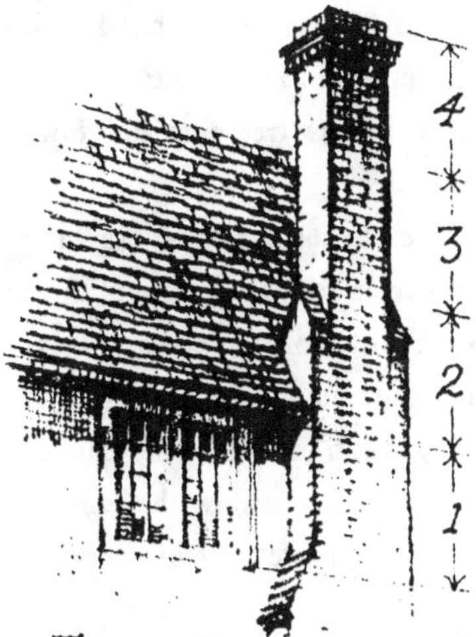

Figure 3

The relative size of shapes must be accurately seen and recorded.

MEASURING PROPORTIONS

The usual and best way of measuring proportions is by the following method. Place the pencil in the hand with the first two fingers behind it, the third and little finger in front, and held firmly by the point of the thumb. The thumb then can work freely up and down the pencil, either in the vertical or horizontal position.

Face the subject to be drawn and decide which proportions are needed, such as the relation of the height of the building to its width, or the height of a doorway to the width of a window. Next, extend the arm and hand as far as possible from the shoulder, close one eye, see that the top end of the pencil is in line with the top or side of the part to be measured, and move the thumb along the pencil until it marks the complete length of this particular feature. By so doing, a definite unit of proportion has been obtained.

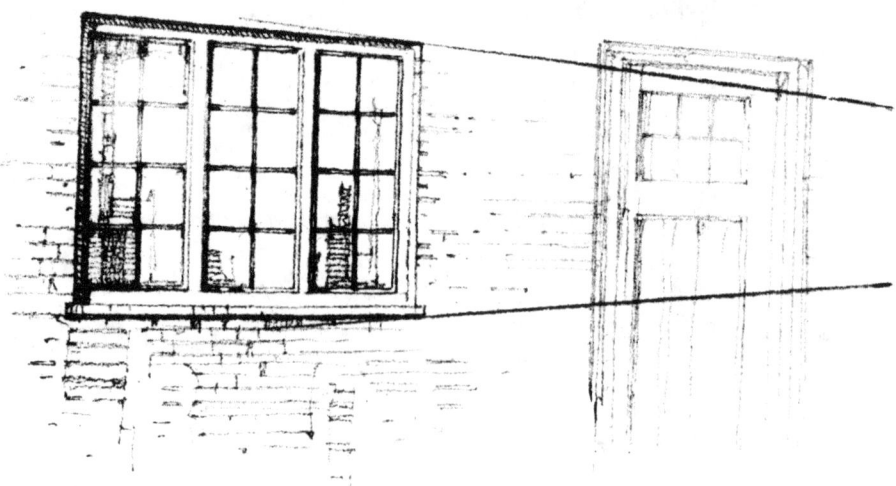

Still with the arm fully extended, and the thumb marking off the given length of pencil, this length may be compared to anything else in view. By way of example, if the height of a window has been measured, it may prove to be but half the height of the doorway, yet almost equal to the doorway's width (see illustration). By this method of using eye and pencil, all the proportions of large planes and small details can be determined, for all spaces and openings are related one to another in terms of measurement.

Through measuring proportions the eye becomes accustomed to gauging them. The time comes when proportions are judged at sight, and set down on paper without taking measurements. Even so, nobody, however skilled, completely discards this system of measuring proportions; it serves well when lines and shapes are unusually complicated, and provides a basis for completed work.

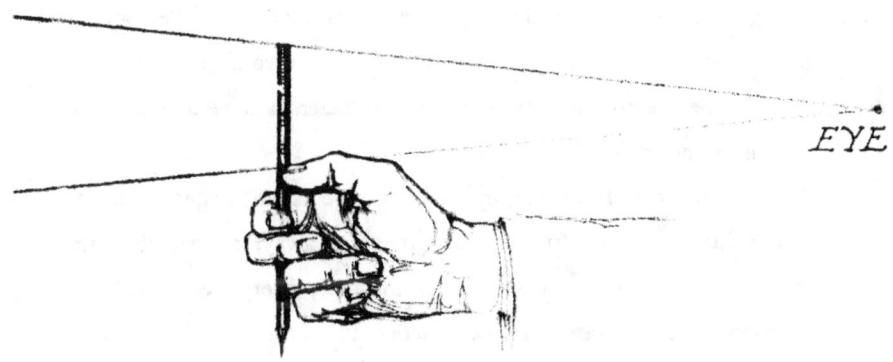

EYE

P E R S P E C T I V E

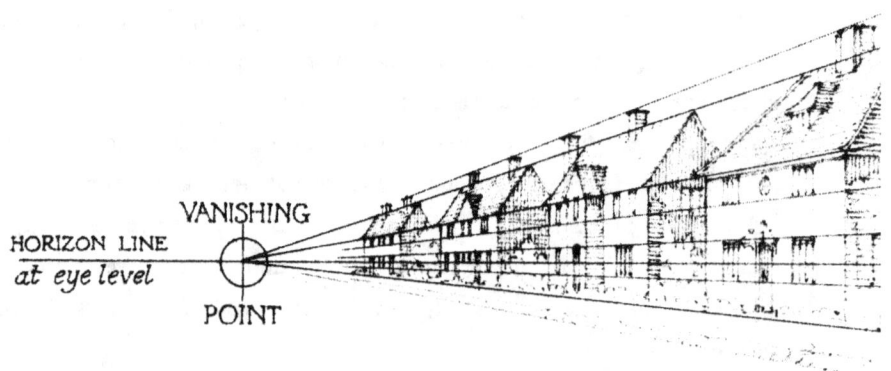

HORIZON LINE
at eye level

VANISHING

POINT

    In rendering buildings, a knowledge of perspective is important. Perspective is the effect of distance upon the appearance of objects. It conforms to definite rules. Although perspective is a large subject, sufficient knowledge of it for use in sketching is not difficult to acquire.

    The effect of distance from the eye causes objects to appear smaller than they actually are. The further they may be away, the smaller they seem to be. In looking down a street, for instance, everyone knows that the more distant houses appear to be smaller than those near at hand,

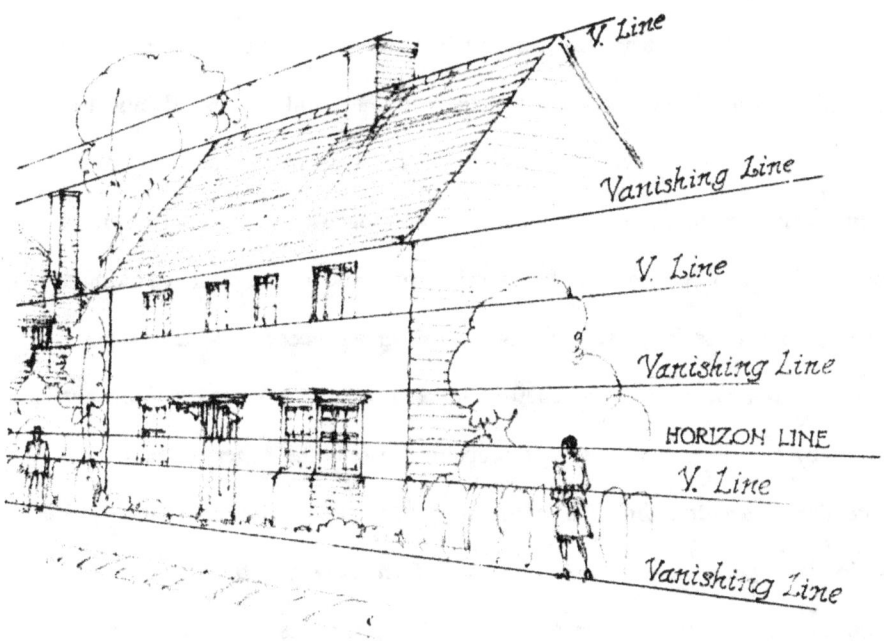

even though the height of each one may be the same. The above diagram illustrates this point.

The reasons which govern these changes in size are indicated by the guide lines marked " horizon line ", " vanishing line ", and the O marked " vanishing point ". These lines, of course, are imaginary ones and not seen ; all of them would meet at one point, the " vanishing point ", which is determined on an imaginary horizontal line that cuts the horizon at the eye level of the spectator, as shewn in this diagram.

21

To obtain the main perspective lines when drawing a house, the pencil may be held at arm's length between the eye and the building. By sloping the pencil in line with the roofs, window-heads, the base of the house, or other features, the various perspective angles can be judged and lightly set down on paper. These will give a basis for carrying the work further while ensuring a general correctness in perspective as the drawing proceeds. When properly observed, all the lines, if continued, would meet at common points in the manner shewn by the diagram below, but probably beyond the edges of the paper. Note also that widths diminish in size by distance; near windows, and such particulars, appear to be wider than those farther away, although the actual dimensions are the same. Correct perspective contributes a good deal towards making a drawing accurate, and here is the effect of right practice, (Figure 4 and opposite).

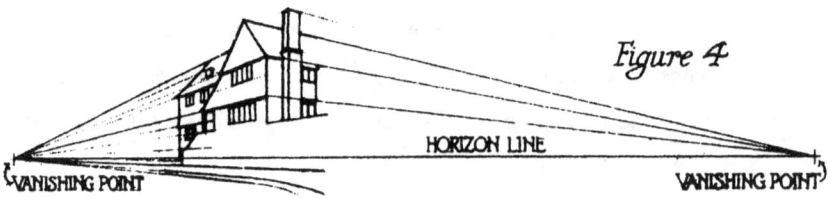

Figure 4

HORIZON LINE

VANISHING POINT

VANISHING POINT

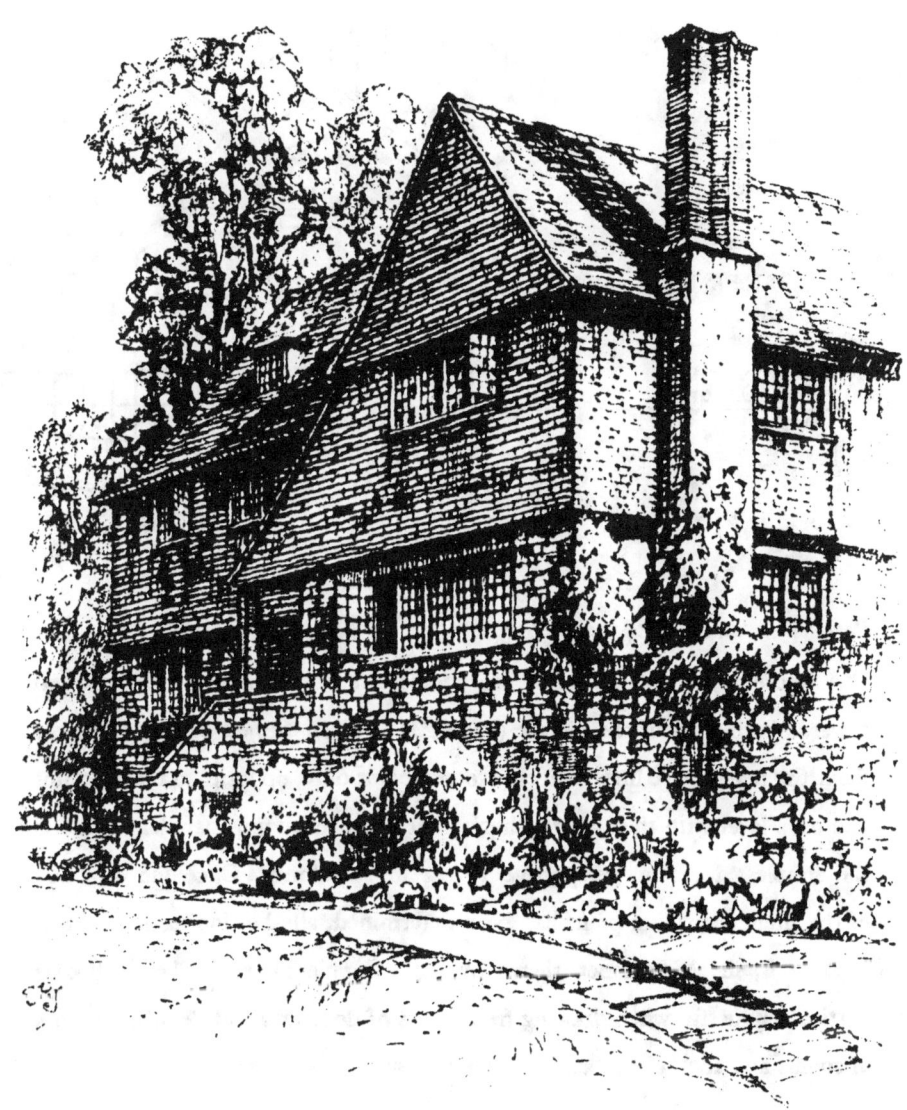

Correct Perspective.

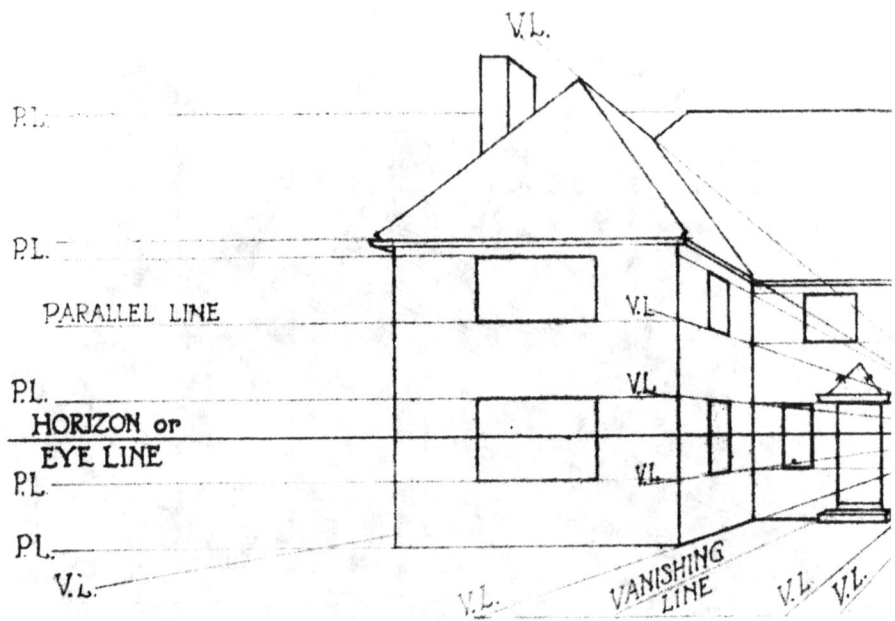

Parallel or ' one point ' perspective.

A house seen from an angle has perspective lines running right and left towards both sides of the picture (Page 23). When viewed exactly from the front the perspective lines converge to one point only, opposite to the spectator and on a level with the eye, the horizontal lines remaining parallel. This is the simplest form of perspective to use in sketching. Once the direction of the single vanishing point has been determined, all the sloping lines direct towards it, in the manner shewn by the example above. The method is particularly useful when drawing front views of doorways and details, interiors of rooms and such things as fireplaces seen at close quarters.

24

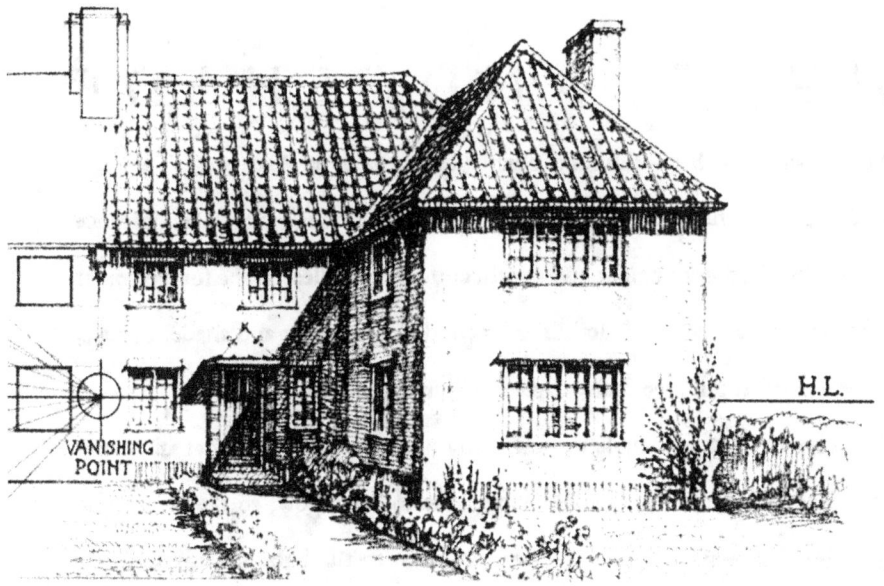

As in judging proportions, so it is with determining perspective. Observation develops the knack of realizing perspective at sight, and drawing it freely without testing by slopes and angles. From early beginnings, the sketcher develops the power to keep in mind these principles which determine the relative values of the near and more distant parts in the drawing. Perspective is observed not only in lines and shapes, but also in tones, colours, and atmosphere. Near details and shadows, for example, may shew stronger than the more distant ones. But I shall say more on this question later on in this book, always remembering that the best interpreter of perspective is the trained eye.

LIGHT AND SHADE

So far we have been thinking chiefly of outlines and shapes. The next consideration is the effect of light and shade which suggests the appearance of depth, in addition to height and width, and offers endless scope for treatment and variety in drawing. Under different conditions of light and shade, a house, or a section of it, can give many choices of subjects for sketching.

The play of light and shade is most easily illustrated by looking at an oblong rectangular box which stands on a table near to a window, so that it may be moved into different positions. When placed with the light striking from the

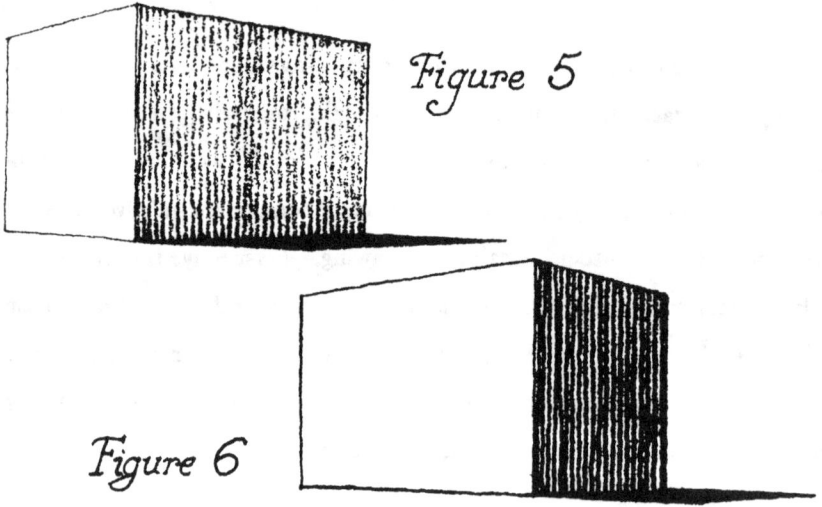

Figure 5

Figure 6

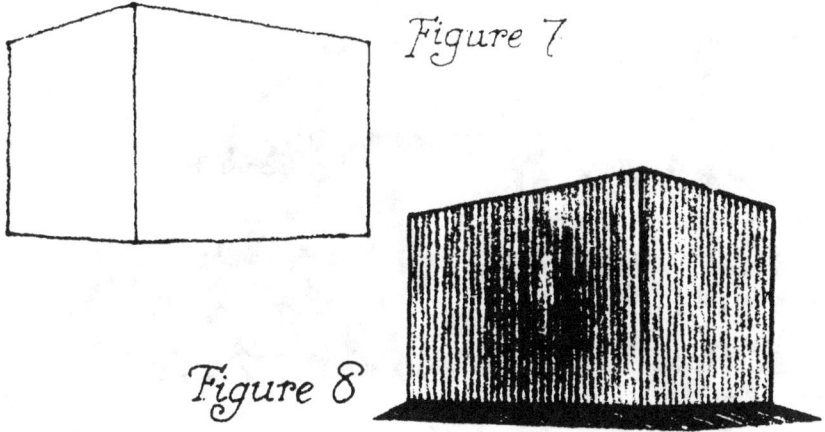

Figure 7

Figure 8

left on to the end of the box, the side is in shadow (Figure 5). Turn the box
round, so that the light strikes the side of it, and the end is in shadow (Figure 6).
In both instances, provided the light from the window is strong enough, a
shadow will be cast on the table from the side or end that is in shade. Next,
make the box directly face the window at an angle shewing both the side and
the end ; by viewing it from the position of the window, the light will be seen
illuminating both surfaces, while the shadow which falls behind on the table
will not be seen at all (Figure 7). Without moving the box, walk round behind
it to observe both end and side in shade, and a shadow from the complete box
cast on the table (Figure 8).

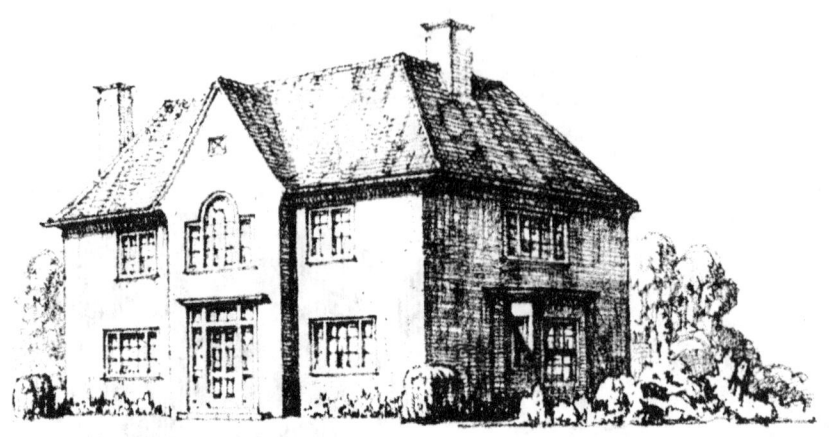

If roofs, doorways, windows, and other particulars are added to the four
sketches of the box, each one then becomes a house. Although the four

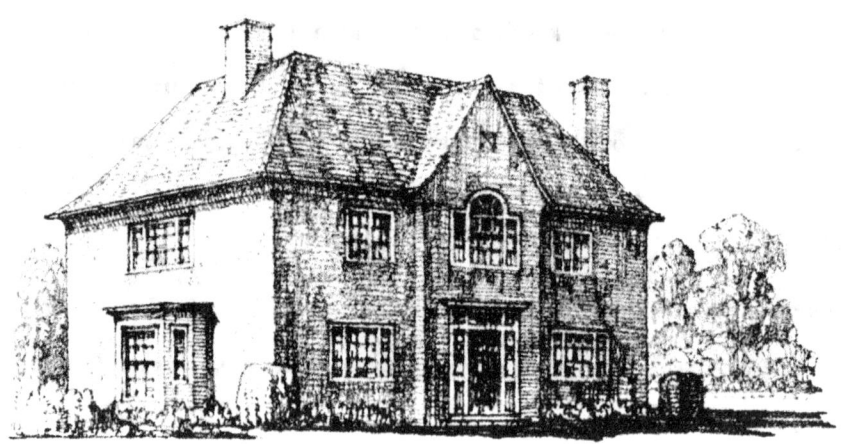

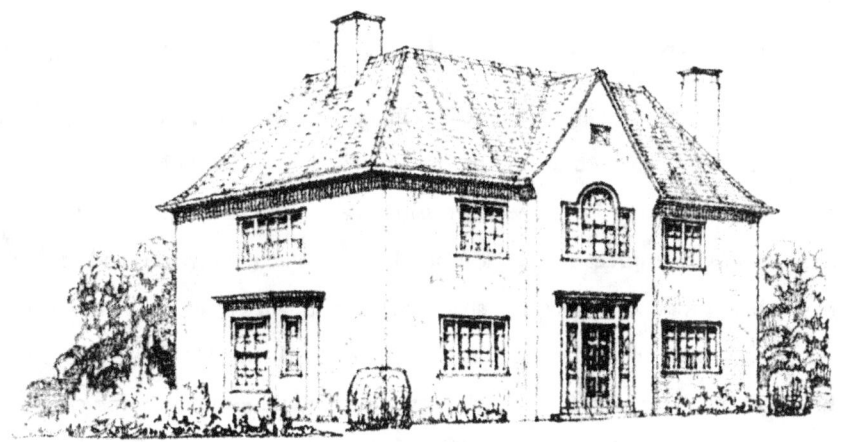

sketches represent the same house, they shew quite different effects due to variations in light and shade, as given by the examples on these pages.

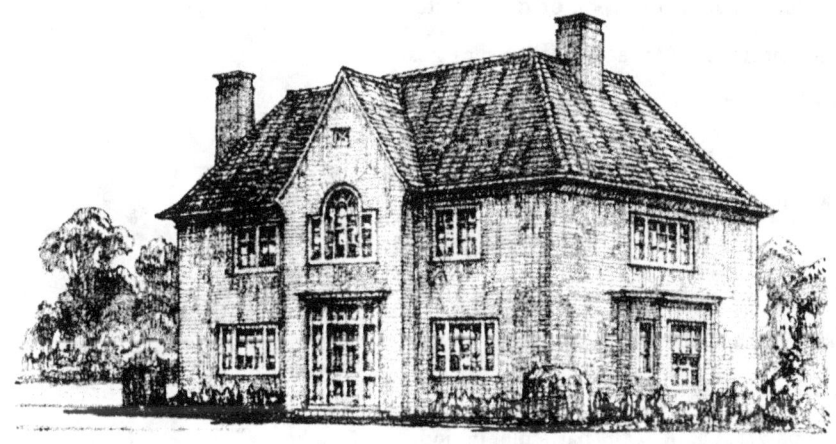

DRAWING THE SHADOWS AND THE

The illustrations just considered demonstrate the elementary and broad appearances of light and shade that are met with in drawing houses. But to the seeing and trained eye the impressions caused by light offer innumerable and unexpected sources for delineation, due to the action of light, and the lack of it which produces shades and shadows. The quality of light differs greatly. Sometimes it is brilliant, sometimes subdued ; all the ranges of light, from bright to dull, from morning to mid-day and on to the evening, bring changed aspects to objects. These have to be studied carefully, and often rapidly, for the angles of the sun's rays never remain fixed. Everyone has watched the sun rise in the early morning and set in the evening. At such times the orb of light

seems to mount up from, or descend to, the horizon. Or again, the sun has been traced through the day apparently progressing slowly through the sky from east to south, and from south to west Throughout the progress, with the angles of light never remaining the same from hour to hour, the shapes and tones of the shadows are determined by the direction and power of light at any particular period.

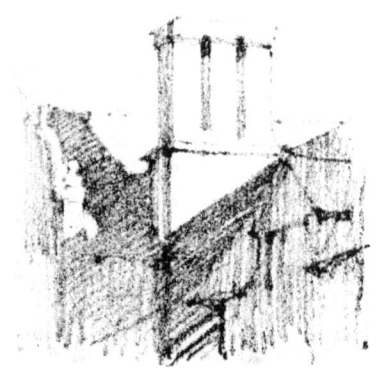

Figure 9

Thus lights and shades, and most

LIGHTS

noticeably out-of-doors, are continually in a state of movement. When drawing them, particularly in sunlight, they should be set down quickly in order the catch the effects before they alter. Have sufficient outlines of the subject drawn

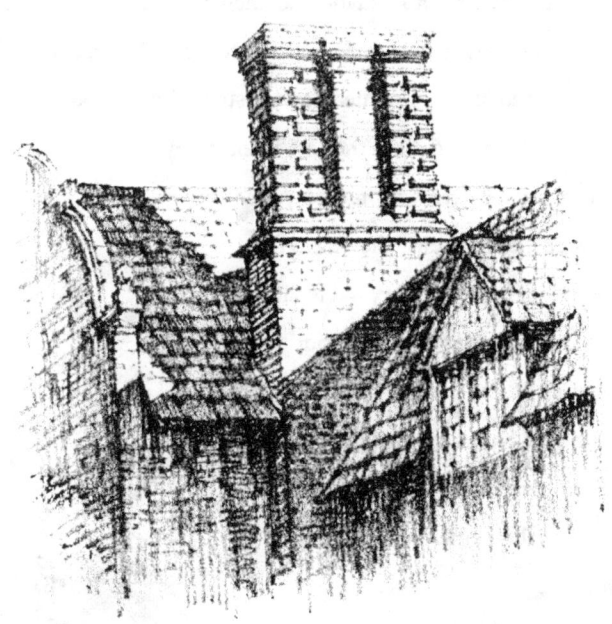

in before the shadows are attempted. Observation will shew that shadows are just as shapely as the parts of the building from which they are cast. Each one, therefore, must be searched out carefully by eye. First sketch them broadly with flat tones (Figure 9). Then add details, noting variations in texture, and the grades of strength caused by reflected light, all of which will become increasingly obvious the more the shadows are studied. In the end, by adding to the first tones broadly indicated, the work will look

31

luminous, just as shadows always do.

Bright surfaces not in shade also shew variety in appearance, due to the play of light. And perspective is demonstrated by the different qualities and colours of near and distant shadows and lights. The more distant they are from the eye, the less detail is seen within them, even though, as sometimes happens, the strength of tone may not vary. Very likely all the lights and shadows cannot be put on paper at one sitting. Rather than hurry, and most likely fail in the task, visit the subject several times at the same hour of day until the work is successfully completed. In the morning, for example, the sun will glint at a sloping angle on to the view ; at mid-day the light will flood downward from overhead ; and in the evening the sloping shadows will make a new set of patterns.

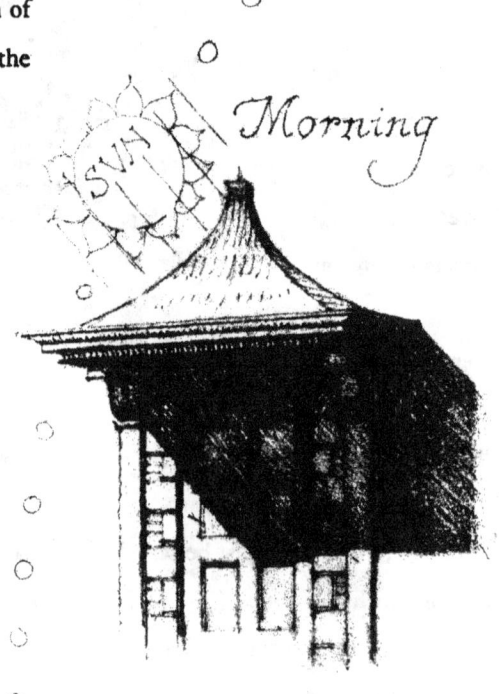

32

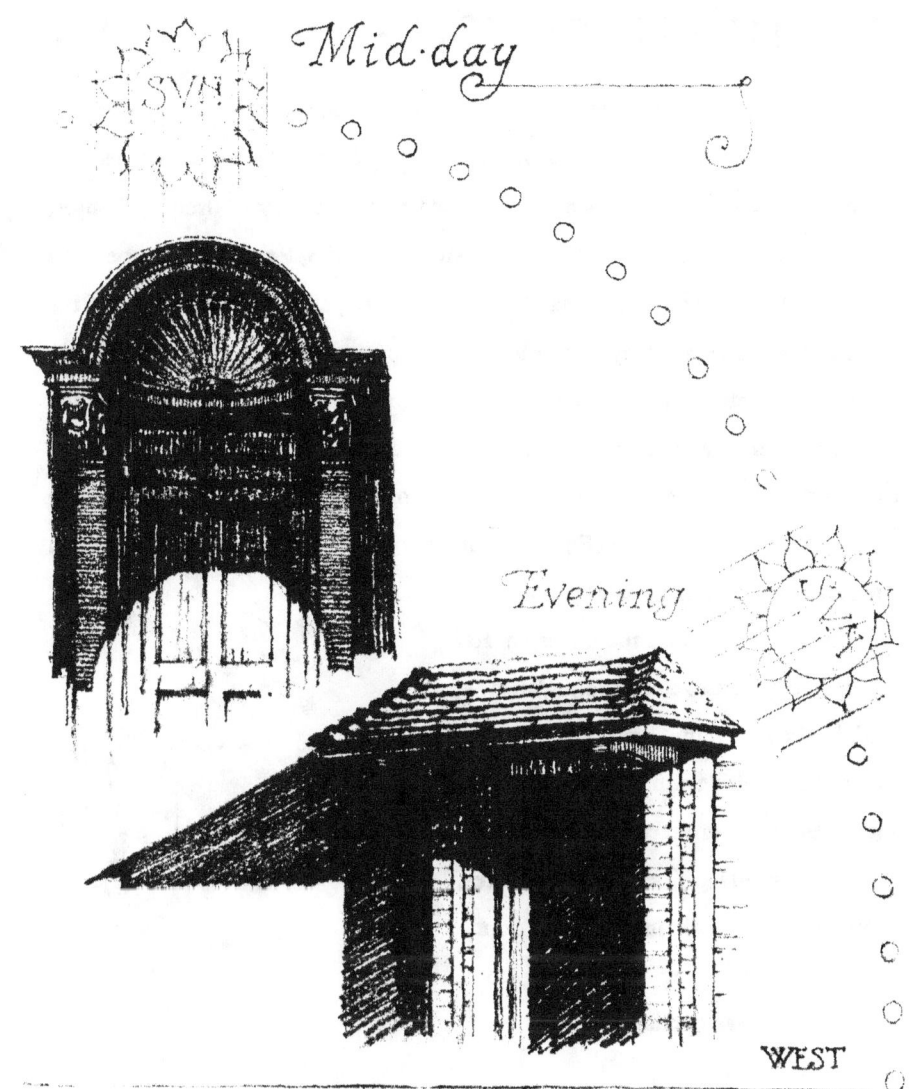

STUDYING THE DETAILS

Practice in using the pencil, and the development of the capacity to see rightly, leads to knowledge of form, proportion, light and shade, and perspective. Perseverance with these essentials will lead to proficiency in drawing houses, and all the particulars belonging to them. The simpler details can be tried first, such as a window or a small fireplace ; in fact, all the separate parts of the house that are seen day by day, either indoors or outside, and which seem likely to offer subjects. The entrance door gives a good position to start with. Study it from different angles, from right and left, and from the front. While drawing, of course, the points which have been mentioned in my previous pages will be remembered and observed (Figures 10 and opposite). With command gained in rendering particular parts of a house, it will be easier to tackle the larger efforts of depicting houses complete, and standing in their surroundings. On the next pages I am giving a number of examples of features common everywhere. Similar ones exist in all localities. Anyone therefore can get to work, just as I have done, and through trying will find both interest and satisfaction.

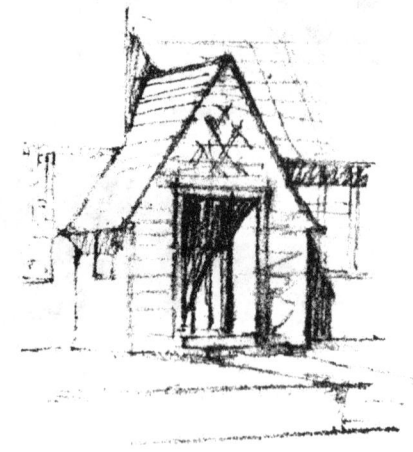

Figure 10

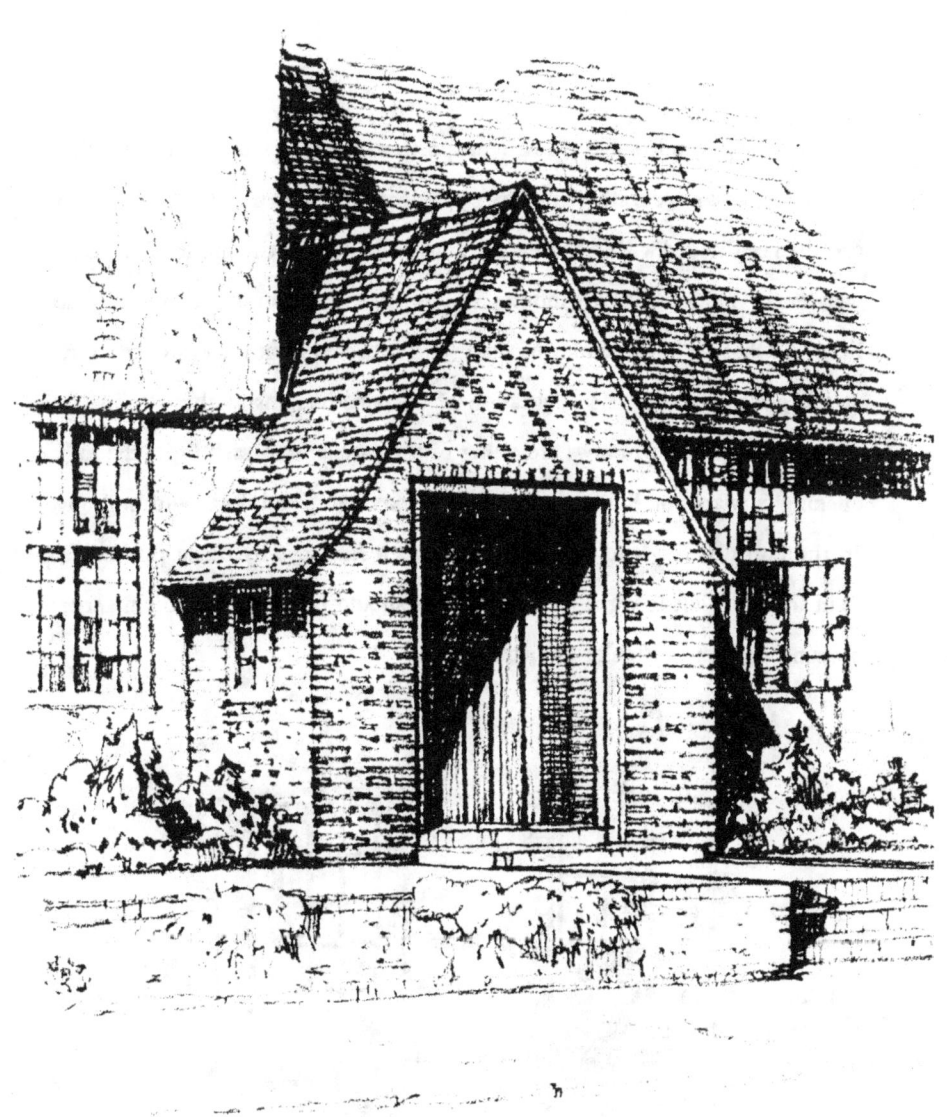

An entrance doorway.

WINDOWS

In drawing windows, the main proportions of the window frames should first be set down accurately in proper perspective. The number of glass panes can then be divided within these main lines. Note that the number of panes in wooden or modern steel windows is less than the number shewn in leaded lights. Observe how the play of shade and reflected light variegates the surface of the glass, and also the suggestion of curtains hanging within, visible from the outside. Most windows are either of the casement or sash type, the former opening outwards on hinges, and the latter moving up and down within grooves. In the north of England windows often open sideways by being pushed from right to left or left to right. These details should be obvious by the manner of drawing in each particular subject.

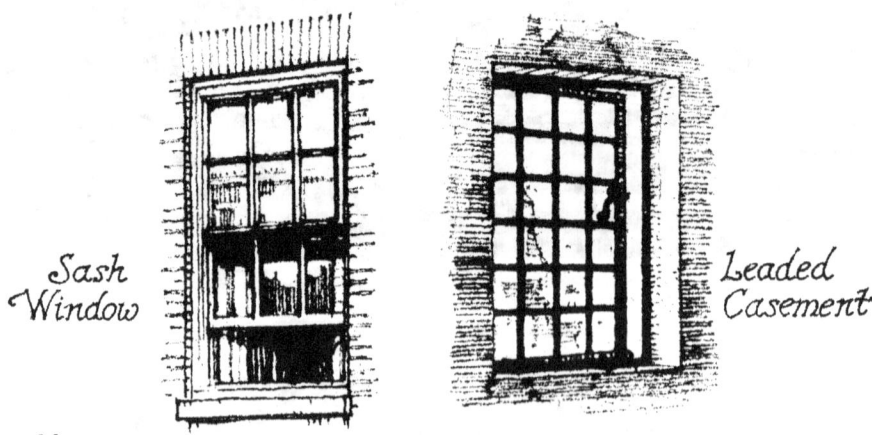

Sash Window

Leaded Casement

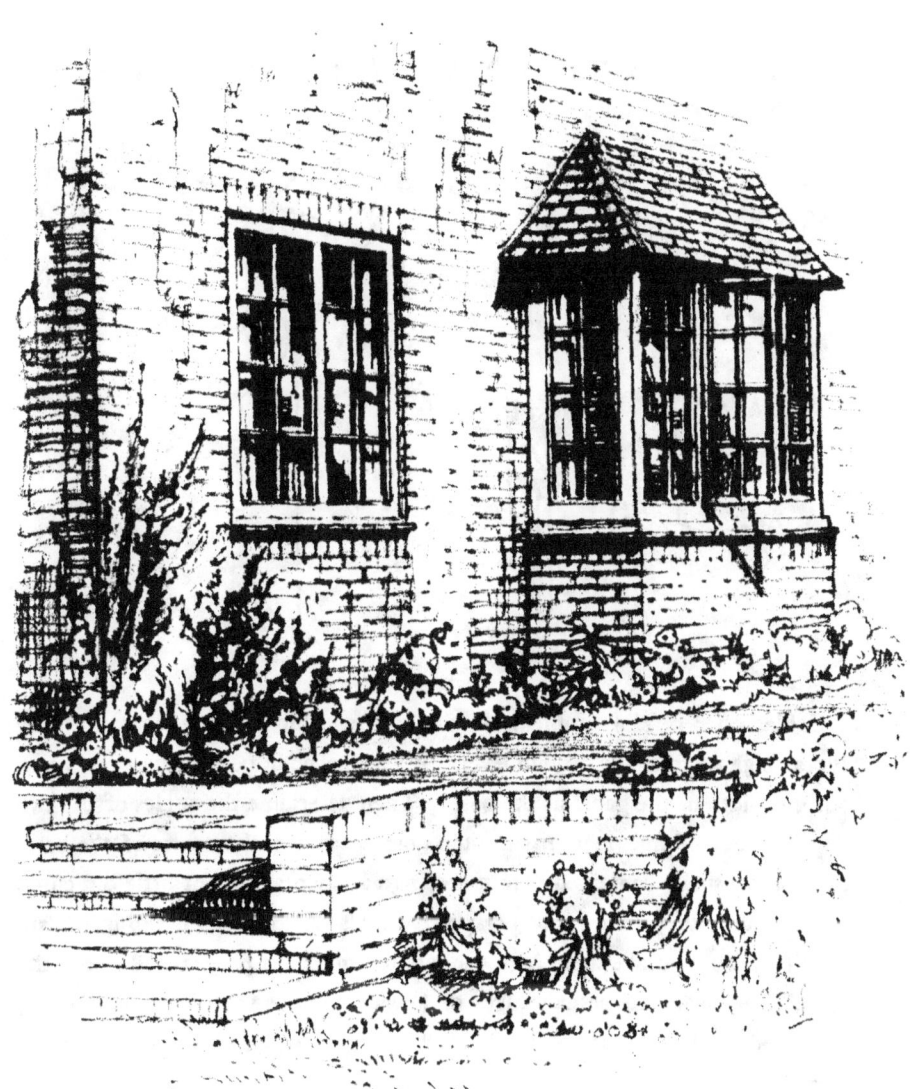

GABLES AND CHIMNEYS

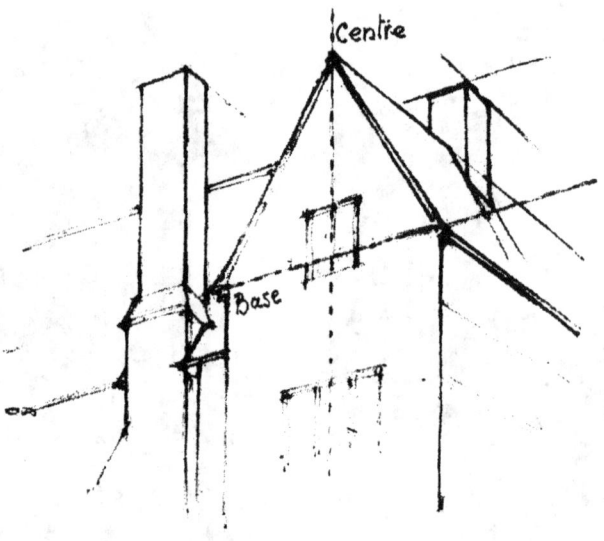

Gables offer certain problems in draughtsmanship because normally they appear high up from the ground level. When viewed in perspective, first mark out the width of the gable at the base. Then determine the angles of the two sloping sides. Remember that the top point rises over the centre of the base. Chimneys, usually contained within rectangular shapes, present little difficulty, for of course they follow the perspective lines of the main building. Care must be taken to make them high enough, for chimneys project well above the roofs, either from the actual ridges or lower down, as shewn in the drawing illustrated. The caps at the heads of chimneys must be observed and drawn carefully.

38

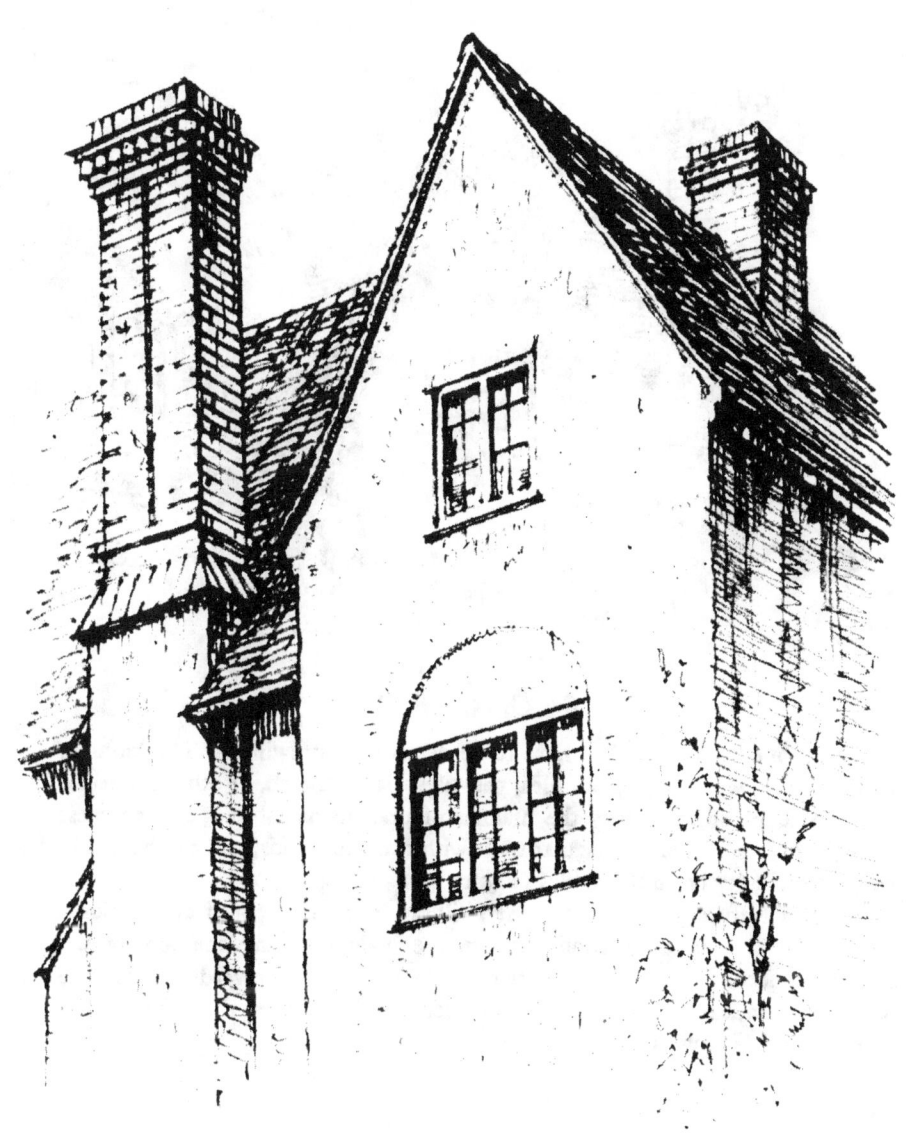

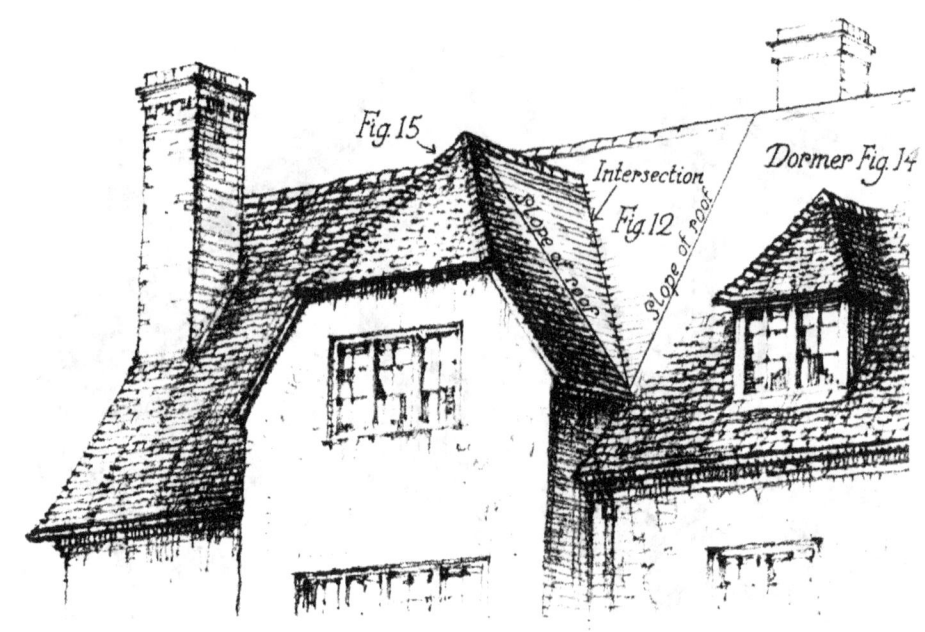

Fig. 15

Fig. 12

Intersection

Slope of roof

Slope of roof

Dormer Fig. 14

R O O F S

Various methods of roofing have to be depicted in drawings. The kinds of roof covering, whether of plain tiles, pan-tiles, slates, thatch, or other materials, also should be suggested by the manner of draughtsmanship. The simplest form of roof rises from rectangular walls with two gable ends, and can be placed without difficulty on to the gables (Figure 11).

Where a feature projects from the building, such as a porch or additional rooms, the line of intersection between the main roof and the roof of the projection needs to be carefully noted. Both roofs slope upwards, so this line of intersection, called a ' valley ', appears somewhere between the sloping angle of each roof (Figure 12).

40

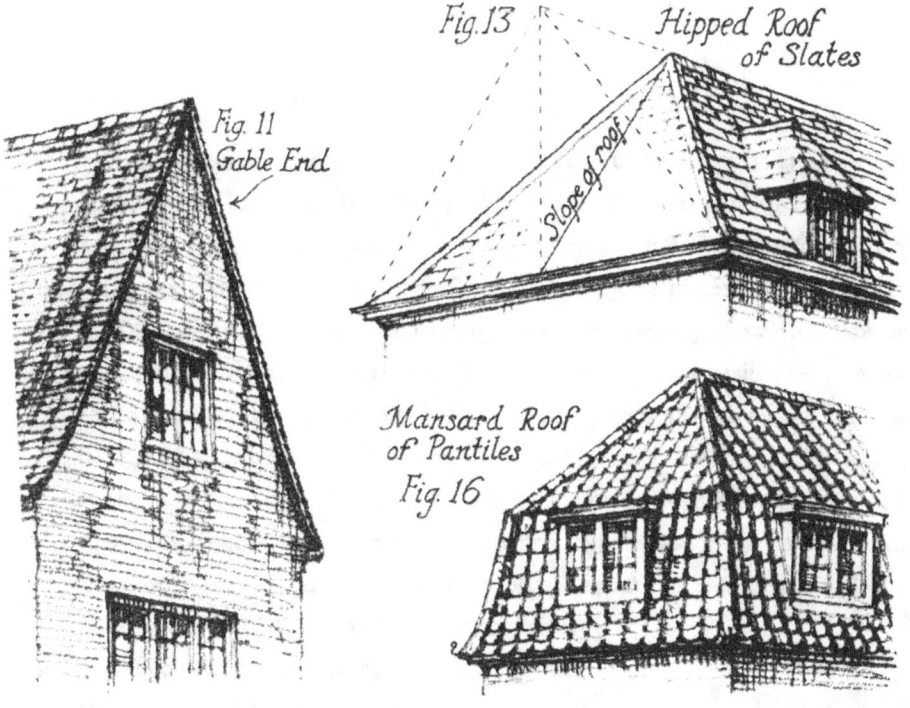

Fig. 11 Gable End

Fig. 13

Hipped Roof of Slates

Slope of roof

Mansard Roof of Pantiles Fig. 16

Hipped roofs, unlike roofs from gables, slope back from the walls on all sides. Intersecting lines at each corner therefore are shewn (Figure 13). Small hipped roofs also are seen over dormer windows (Figure 14), or cutting off the top point of a gable (Figure 15). In drawing all hipped roofs, the most important points to determine are the sloping angles of the surfaces and the lines of intersections.

Mansard roofs have two sloping surfaces. The lower portion rises steeply from the walls, and the upper section is formed by an ordinary hipped roof (Figure 16). Here again, the angles of the surfaces, and the intersecting lines at the corners, must be accurately observed. The Mansard type provides the maximum area inside roofs.

41

CURVED FEATURES

The parts of houses which are made up of curved surfaces should be sketched freely as they appear to the eye, and be persevered with until they convey a correct appearance. But it is well to know the principle that governs the shapes of circles when seen in perspective. The limits of circles are contained within squares; drawn in perspective, these squares are marked SQ on the diagrams below. The diagonals of the squares, DD, give central points C at the intersection. Lines passing through these points C provide the central limits of the circles, EE. On these guide lines the shapes can be formed. Additional perspective lines, AA, will further help towards accuracy. The circular windows illustrated on the opposite page, and also the curved bow-window and steps which are segments of circles, could be determined in the above manner.

Actually they were drawn freehand from observation. This is the right method to develop; only for guidance have I mentioned the principle governing circles in perspective. The disposition of light and shade, and the drawing of the shadows, are important particulars in suggesting the roundness of curved surfaces.

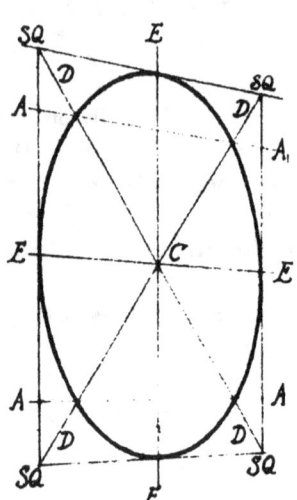

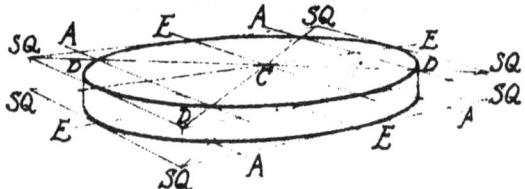

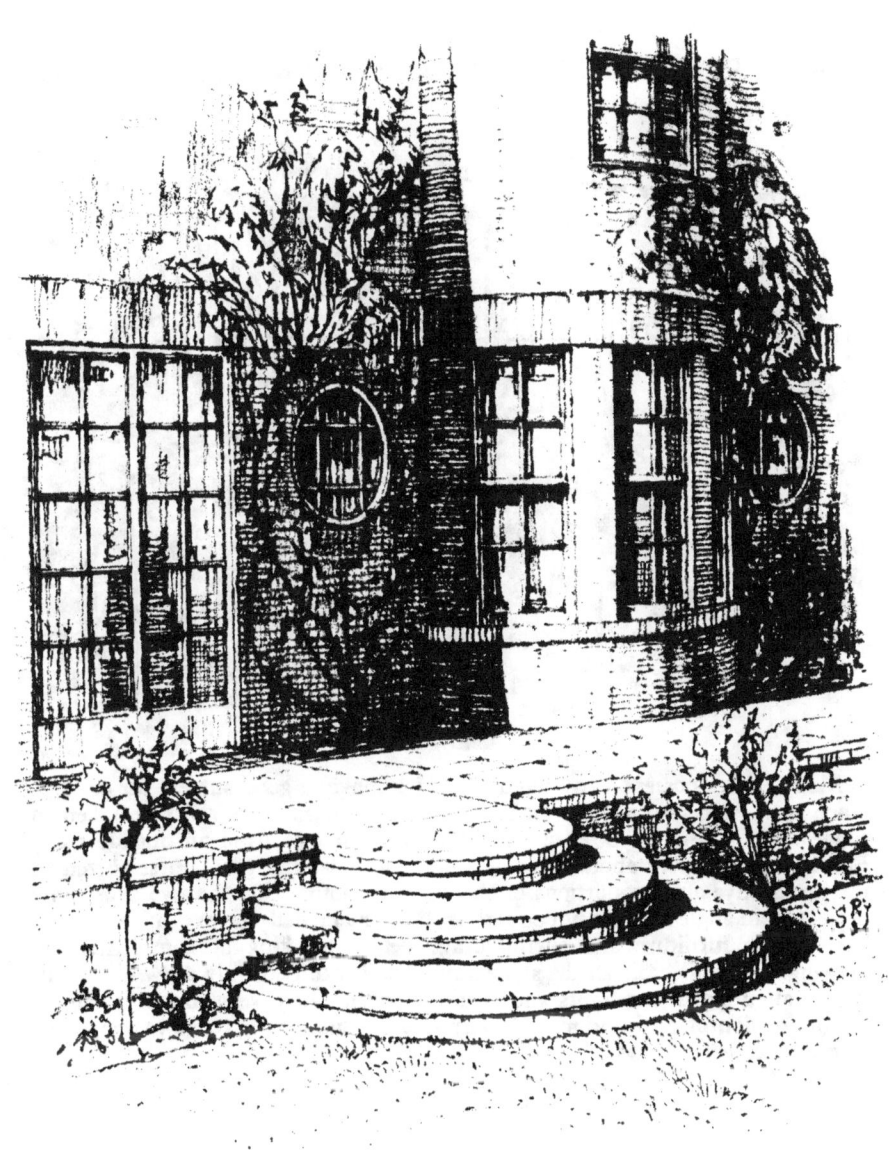

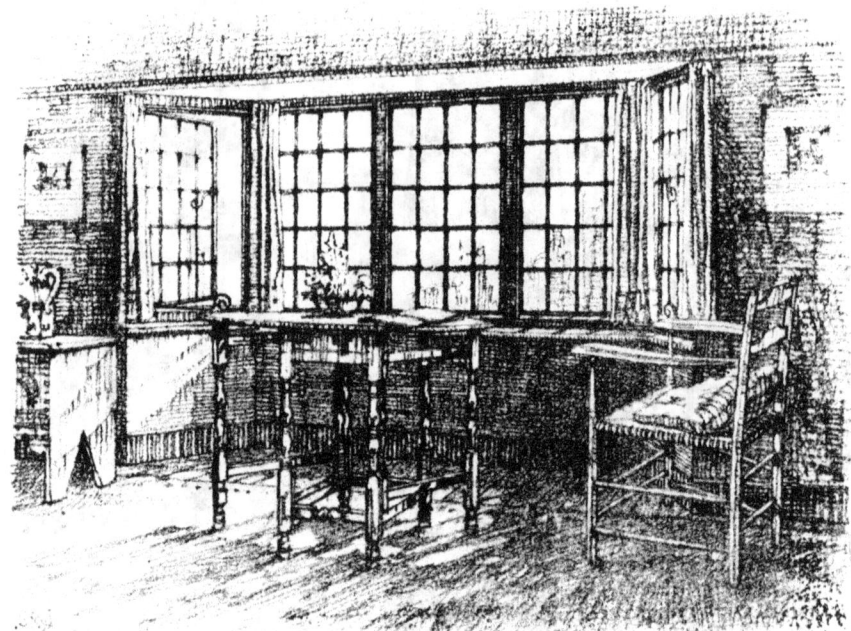

Many houses possess a bay-window, which makes a good subject for practice when seen from the inside. In a feature such as this care must be taken to suggest the " inside " look, which differs in character from an outside view. But I shall say more about drawing interiors on later pages. First sketch in the perspective and proportions of the window, noting that the two side lights project at an angle and are not square with the main wall. Next, mark out the lines of the furniture and surroundings before thinking of completing the drawing. On this basis all the shapes and details can be firmly drawn in. Pay special attention to the lights and shadows as they help very much to convey the impression of an interior. Usually interior subjects have more weight of tone than exterior views.

FIREPLACES

Anyone can try a hand at drawing fireplaces because all houses possess them. They offer plenty of variety in shape and appearance, and being indoors, they come in well for wet and cold days when sketching outside is impossible. To get the general main lines on to paper, proceed in the same way as mentioned on the opposite page in connection with the bay-window. Fireplaces are of many kinds and shew all sorts of materials, including wood, iron, stone, marble, tiles, and bricks. The character of these materials should be suggested by differences in actual drawing. The combinations of forms and tones often give good decorative effects. The Dutch tiles shewn in my illustration, for example, make an effective centre for the surrounding woodwork and panelling. Light from fires, especially at dusk or in the evening, often helps to make good fireplace pictures.

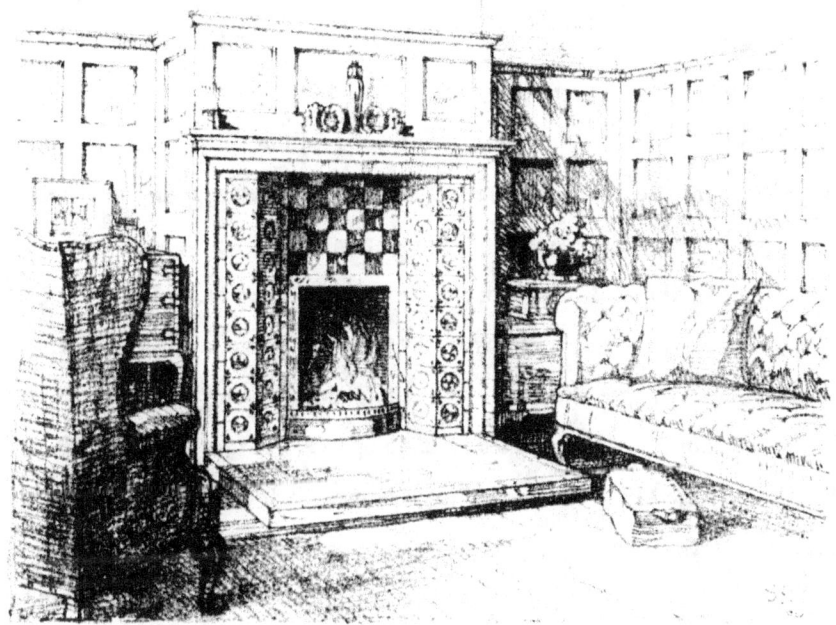

COMPOSITION

That a drawing shall look well as a picture, and suggest the character of the subject it represents, depends very much on its general scheme and plan, that is, its composition. This question of composition is a first thought in making a drawing, and a last thought in completing it. The way the main lines hang together, and thus " compose ", the balance of tones, and the suppression of parts, where necessary, in order to give accent to leading passages of interest, mean a great deal in results achieved. Good composition amplifies the qualities of draughtsmanship ; it helps to convey impressions formed in the mind ; it makes all the different parts of a drawing combine into one complete whole.

In the higher planes of picture-making composition is an advanced study. Its scope is infinite. The most experienced artists never realize the limits. Nature is the greatest exponent of composition. The fields, the woods and the hills, the rhythm and balance of tree forms, shapes and harmonious arrangements shewn by flowers, patterns made by light and shade, and the wonders of the changing skies, are the best masters for both drawing and composition, whether the aim is to depict houses or anything else. A fine painter and friend of mine, Sir Alfred East, never failed to carry his sketch book with him in order to set down arrangements of composition whenever seen. " If you do not note them when you find them ", he used to say, " you may never see them again ".

And our great genius, J. M. W. Turner, was known as the little man always with a pencil and sketch book, with which he made thousands and thousands of studies.   For the beginner, as well as the expert, no better example could be followed.

I mention the above matters because composition, even if it may offer difficulties, is well worth perseverance.   A little knowledge of it can improve drawing efforts immensely ; it is exciting to arrange in one's own work ; and an appreciation of it helps tremendously when looking at the work of great artists, as everyone who draws should do, for then it can be discovered how they built up their fine effects.   In the space at my disposal I can but briefly touch on this subject.   Much more can be learned by trying, and by developing the natural taste, and the ability for gaining knowledge, with which everyone is endowed in more or less degree.

Some of the broad essentials for managing composition, and which should be remembered when drawing, are now given.

1.   Selection of the point of view and the grouping need care, as already mentioned on pages 12 to 15.

2.   Aim for simplicity.   Seek out the general arrangements of the lines, and the broad effects of tone.   Even when the view appears full of complications, the main divisions of it are not complex ; the thousands of leaves of a tree, for instance, or the many bricks in a wall, are included within a few definite shapes.

PROGRESS IN COMPOSITION

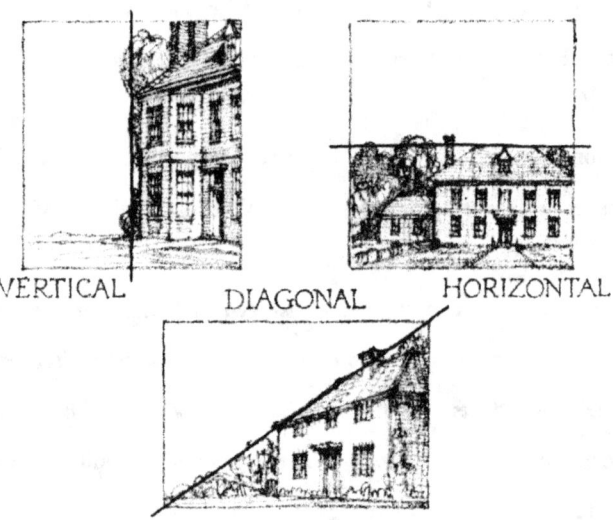

VERTICAL DIAGONAL HORIZONTAL

3. Equal proportions that cut the picture into two halves should be avoided. Arrangements divided equally, whether in the vertical, horizontal, diagonal, or other directions, look obvious, dull, and lacking in variety.

4. Mark the contrasts between light and dark passages of the subject.

Contrast is effective.

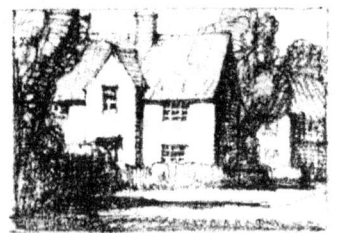

48

These bring interest and emphasis to drawings.

5. Carefully draw detail where it is needed to give importance to particular features. Where less emphasis is required, subdue the details, or only lightly suggest them.

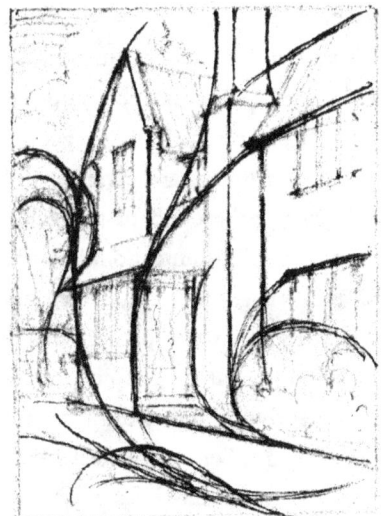

Consider the composition lines.

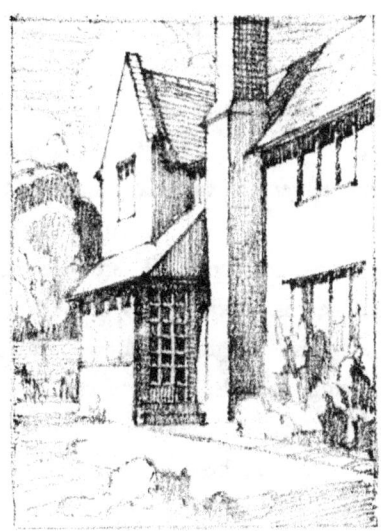

Drawings should exhibit pattern.

6. Keep in mind the pictorial pattern made by the work as a whole. The arrangement of the lines, together with the disposition of lights, tones, and dark shadows in a drawing should exhibit a satisfactory and complete pattern, in addition to representing the subject depicted. Good drawings always demonstrate this feeling for pattern.

COMPOSITION

Art conceals art. The method by which a composition has been made should not stand out conspicuously. Though harmony, variety, gradation, and contrast, when carefully planned, can determine good effects, these factors in composition ought not to appear studied or obvious. If they do, the means employed, rather than the result desired, will be too dominant; further, the direct and natural expression in drawing will suffer. The example opposite illustrates some of the points which have been mentioned. The general arrangement of the lines, and the broad system of pattern, are given on the preceding page 49. Main lines flow upward from the ground to the gable, chimney, and roofs. These give the suggestion of a solid foundation, balance, and height. Other lines of walls, windows, and foliage repeat and continue the theme. Lights, shadows, and textures contribute to the pattern of the drawing, and also provide variety. The bay-window, gable, and chimney—central features of the subject—are given importance through exhibiting the contrasts of highest lights and deepest darks, the shades being strongest round the doorway to the bay. In regular gradation the tones and lines reach the edges of the drawing. The texture of the building is shewn by the rough-cast walls, frames and glazing of the windows, the slate roofs, and the upper brickwork of the chimney. Foliage and flowers convey the idea of the setting. Shadows and white clouds help to give the aspect of sunlight. But these surroundings, whether firmly rendered or but lightly indicated, lie in secondary relation to the main subject; they are not powerful enough to lead the eye away from the central motive of the drawing, which is the house, though standing in a garden.

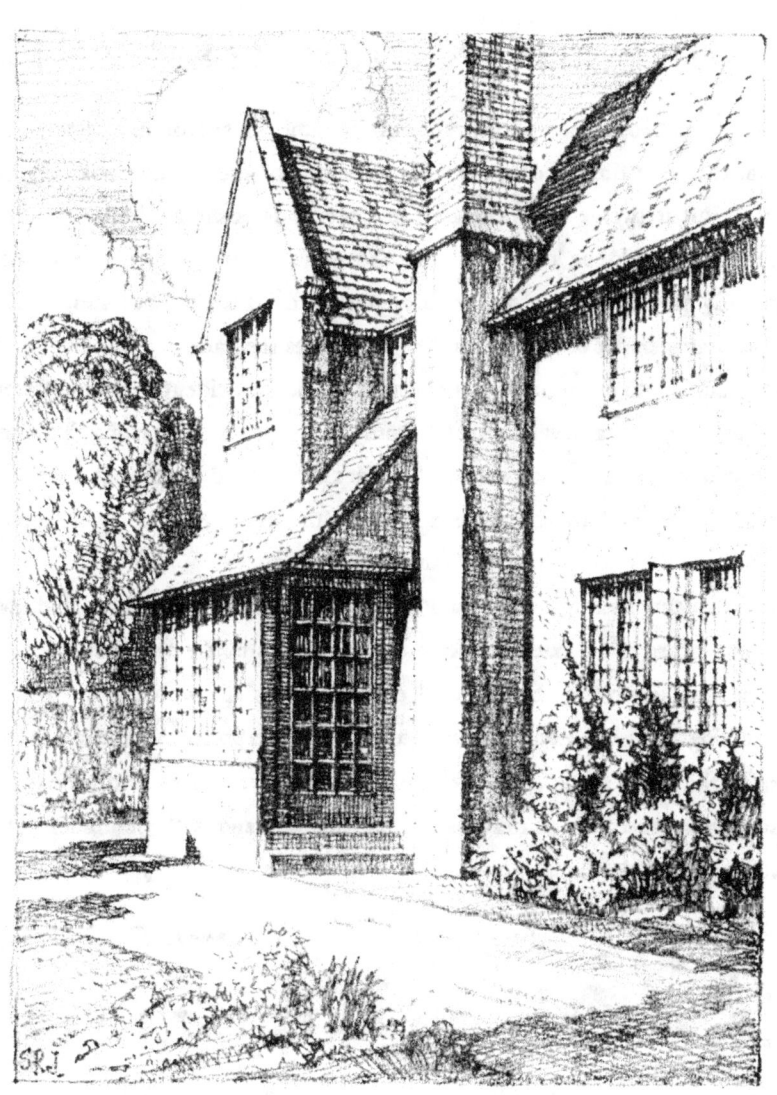

EXPRESSION IN DRAWING

If a dozen people took photographs of the same house from the same position, and at the same time of day, the twelve results obtained would look very much alike. But if twelve people made drawings under exactly similar conditions, each result would be different from the other. One picture might depend especially on the handling of linework, another on the effect of tones, or a third on the management of detail; in other examples the various qualities suggested by the subject to each individual observer would be evident. Such differences in effort arise, in a great measure, from " expression in drawing " which, in relation to external objects, reveals through skill of hand the thought, sentiment, or feeling, aroused by things seen through the eye. And no two people set down what they see in just the same way.

Individuality therefore plays an important part in expression through drawing. Just as clothes to an extent indicate the characters of the wearers, so qualities of line and touch are the personal expressions of all who draw. They are connecting links between objects seen and the interpreters of them. It is not wise to think too much about expression in the early stages of drawing. The best way to proceed is to draw as well as possible, and with the understanding that naturally develops while the pencil works on the paper. Skill and

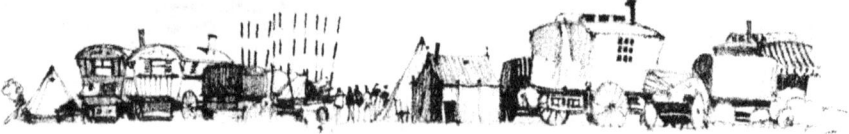

Gipsies' houses, Epsom Downs

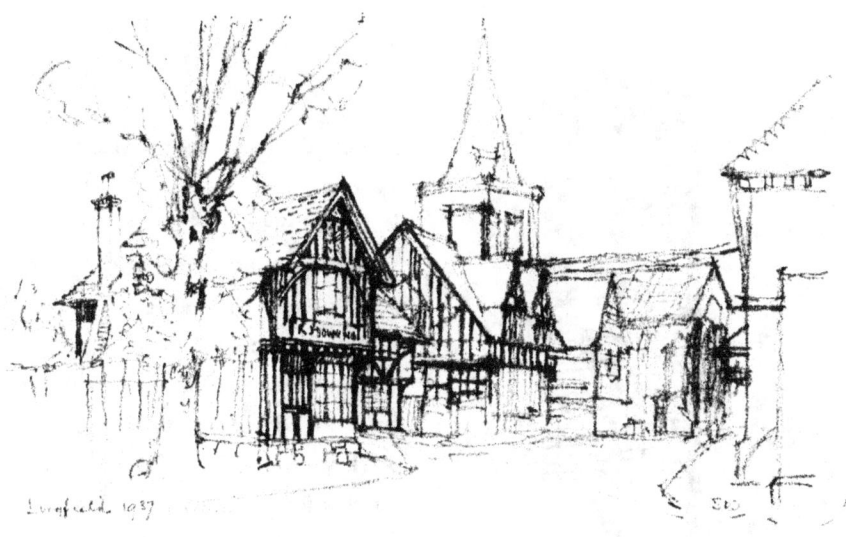

expression develop together. In course of time each one who tries will gradually find the best ways and means for personal expression in drawing. The accompanying sketches demonstrate my own interpretations of things observed, rapidly set down in my sketch book in my particular way.

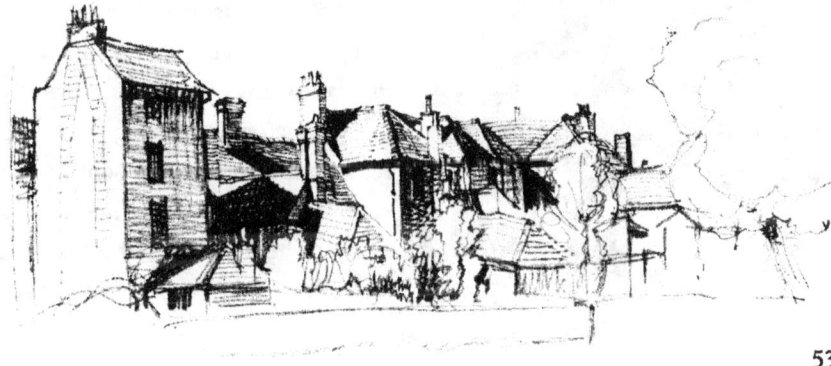

53

SURFACE

The distinct characteristics of the various materials of buildings also influence the expressive use of line and form in drawing houses. Bricks, timber, plaster, and the range of substances that made up houses, give changes in surface textures. These various textures have to be represented by expressive work and touch. Through careful observation, and with skill gained by eye and hand, even single lines can be made to suggest either brickwork, stone, or other building materials. The contrasts evident between new and old buildings again demand expression in drawing.

By way of example, I am giving two instances of brickwork, because many of us live in brick houses and everybody possesses a chimney. Figure M represents a modern chimney built not many years ago. The lines are true and straight ; the bricks and mortar-joints are clean and sharp. Altogether it

Figure M

54

TEXTURES

appeared to me as a nice chimney of a pleasant house, and I have tried to express it as such.

The chimney of Figure N is a very old one, erected hundreds of years ago. But it is still a good chimney, not a bit tumble-down, and continues to serve its purpose well. It makes known the changes of Time, and the way in which men built before everybody thought so much about machinery. Age and weather have played little tricks with the brickwork and mortar-joints. So in my drawing I have endeavoured to suggest what I discovered when looking at this old chimney.

It does not matter a bit whether one prefers new buildings to old ones, or the reverse. Each should be given its own mode of expression. And if the chimneys had been built of stone, or faced with plaster, they would have suggested quite different interpretations.

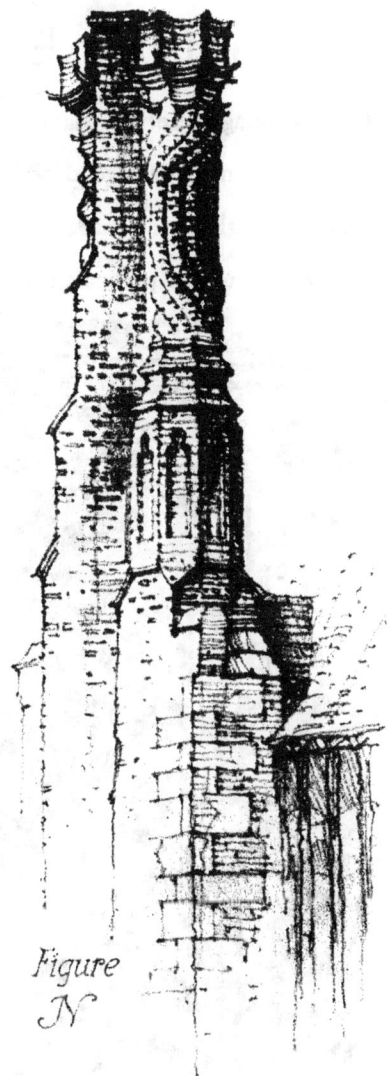

Figure N

INTERIORS

I am devoting these last pages to drawing interiors, for the insides of the
rooms we live in figure a good deal in our lives. And before I get down to
this subject, perhaps my reader would like to peep at the room in which I
have thought out the particulars to put into this book. So here it is, just

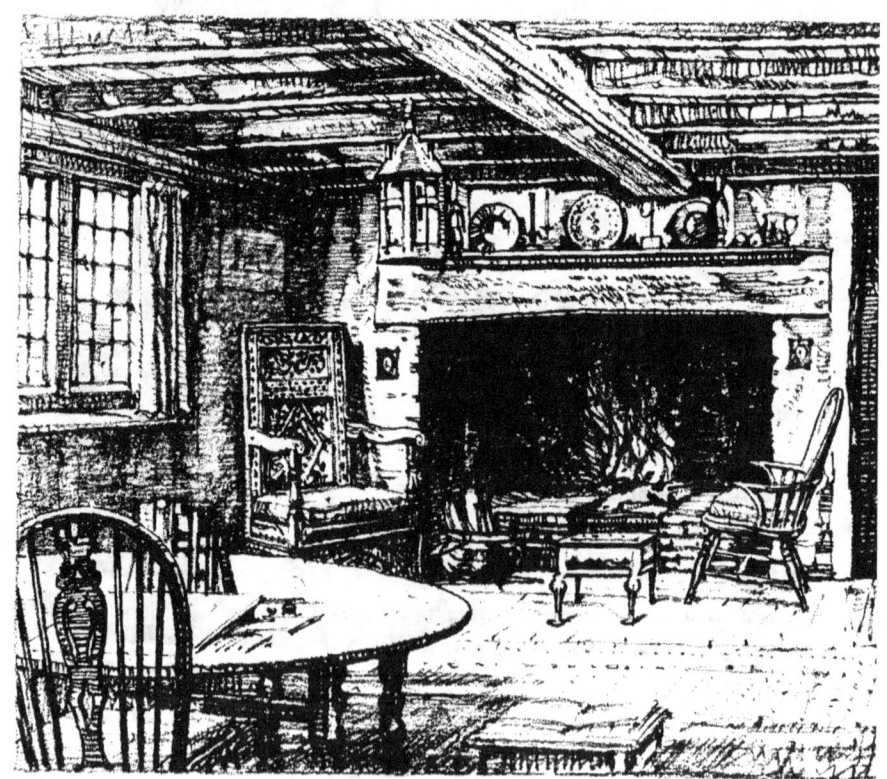

below, drawn in crayon.

I hope my drawing makes you feel that this is an old room. I like to live in old houses, and possibly this one was built when Queen Elizabeth knew Sir Francis Drake, or perhaps not very long afterwards. It can be very cosy, either when the sun shines through the windows in summer, or with the fire

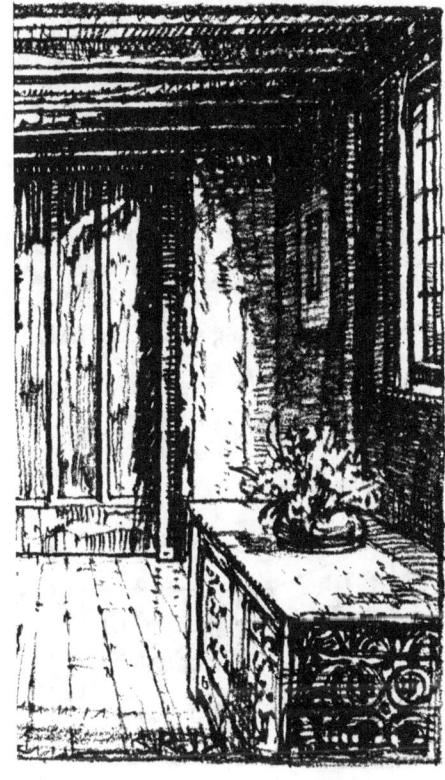

sparkling up the wide chimney on winter nights and reflecting on the beams and woodwork. It also suits my old family possessions which you can see by the furniture and oddments. But new rooms can be just as attractive, though in a different way; in fact, I built another house for myself, and you can see a window and a fireplace from it on pages 44 and 45. Anyone therefore can have great fun by drawing their own rooms, whether new or old, and putting in the furniture and things, when friends may say, " Oh, that's

INSIDE THE ROOMS

just like it ! " or perhaps that it isn't, which means we must try all over again !

Drawing interiors of houses is very similar to depicting exteriors, only, one might say, the other way about. On pages 26 and 27 I have compared the simple outside lines of a house to a rectangular box. As room interiors usually are rectangular in shape, they may be similarly considered ; but with this difference, that the *inside* of the box is viewed, in the manner shewn by the two diagrams below.

After the point of view has been carefully chosen, the main proportions and perspective lines are set down lightly on the paper. With this basis the details then can be filled in. The same idea may be applied all over the house—in the living-rooms and bedrooms see pages 60 and 61 overleaf), and in the hall, though with this last subject the slope of the staircase, and the gradual rise of the stairs, must be closely observed when sketching, as indicated by the drawing on the opposite page.

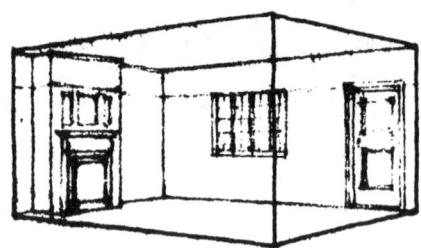 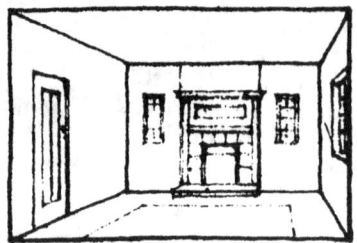

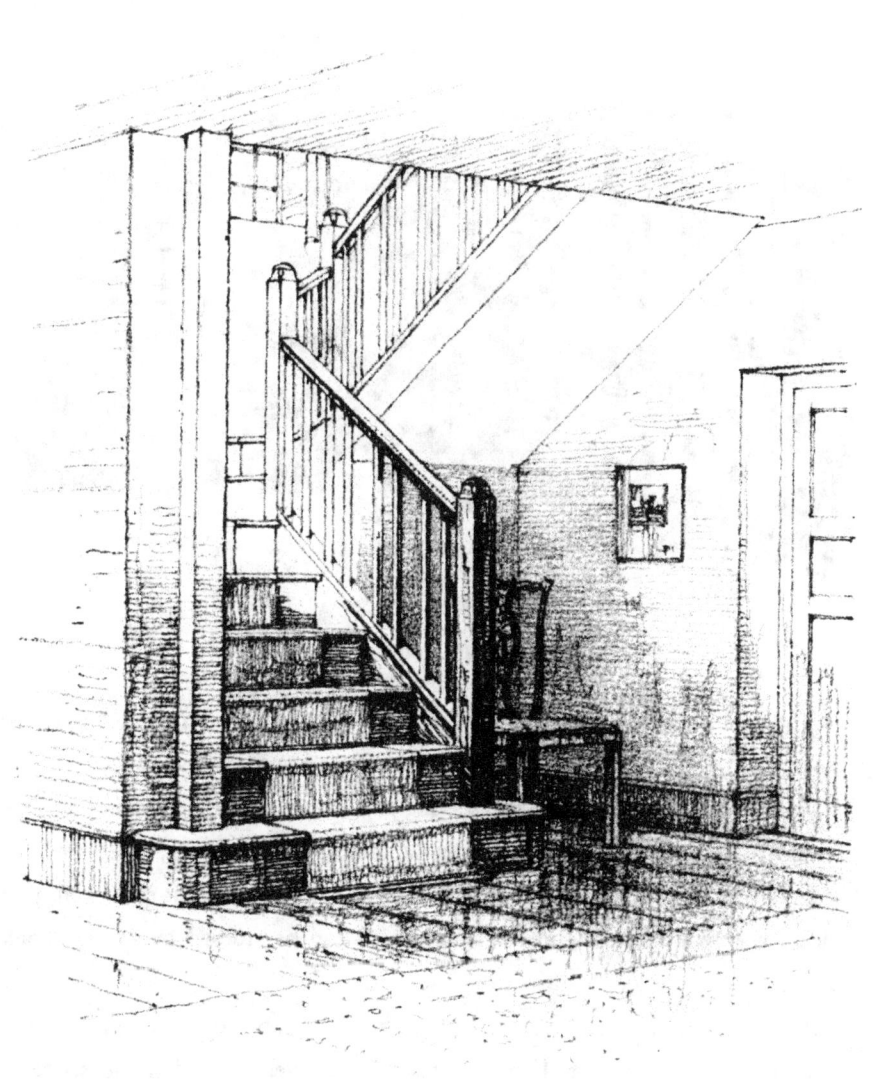

Hall and Stairs—not completed.

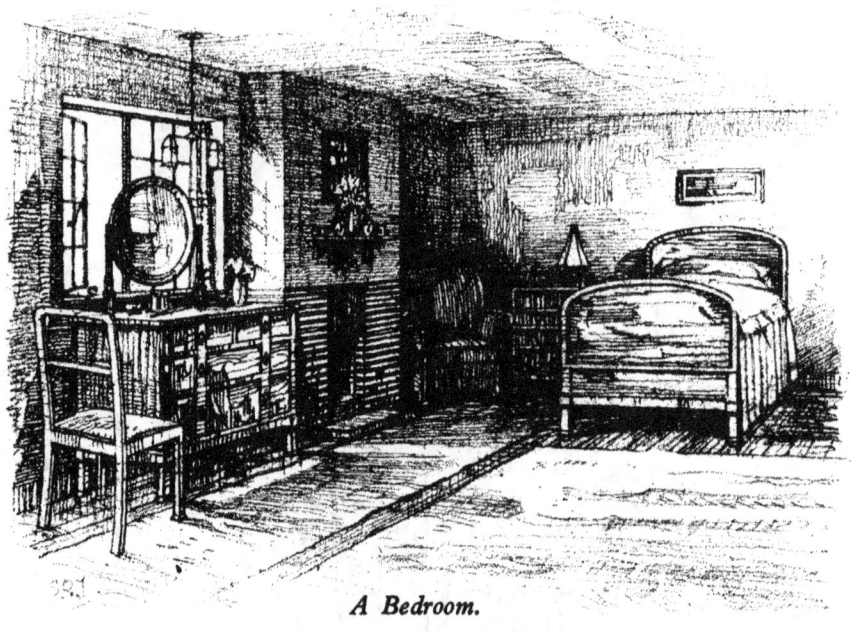

A Bedroom.

The furniture and accessories have to be drawn just as carefully as the actual rooms, and on the same principles of proportion and perspective that previously have been pointed out. In representing the interiors of rooms it is therefore necessary to acquire the knack of drawing tables, chairs, settees, vases, flowers, and all sorts of objects that make up a home. If people are put in as well, that means a knowledge of figure drawing, which can be studied by another book of this series entitled, " How to draw Portraits ".

All the interests and things that centre round the places we live in can fall into the scheme of pictorial representation. In every direction the scope is unlimited, and intimate associations enhance the pleasures of drawing.

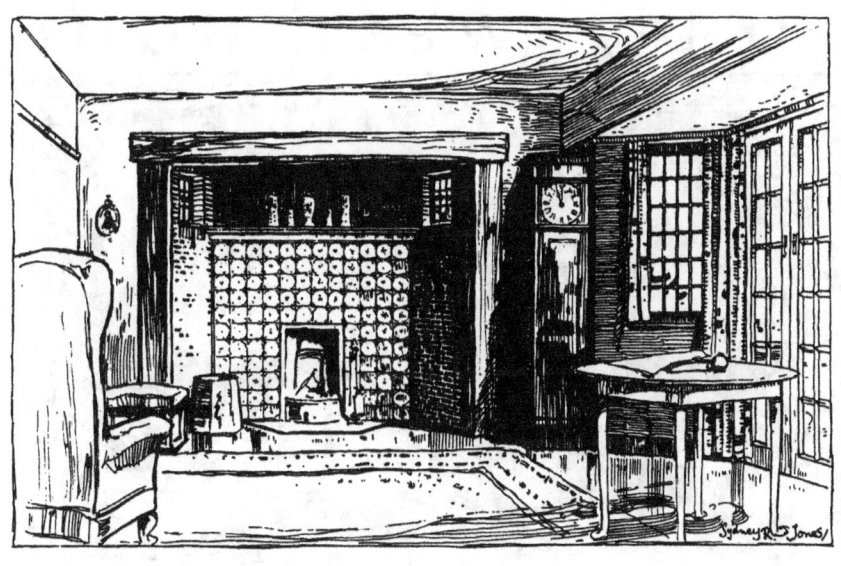

A Living Room.

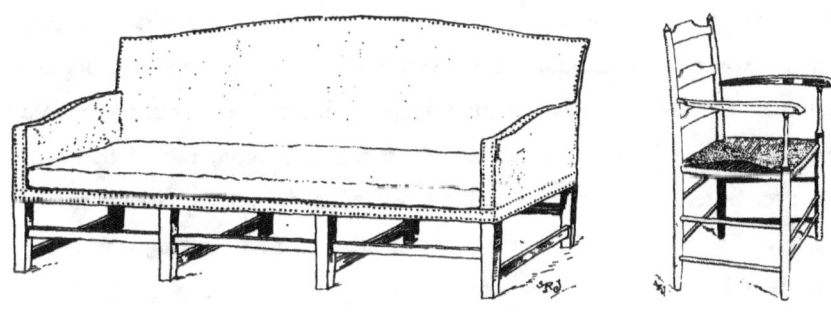

HOME SWEET HOME

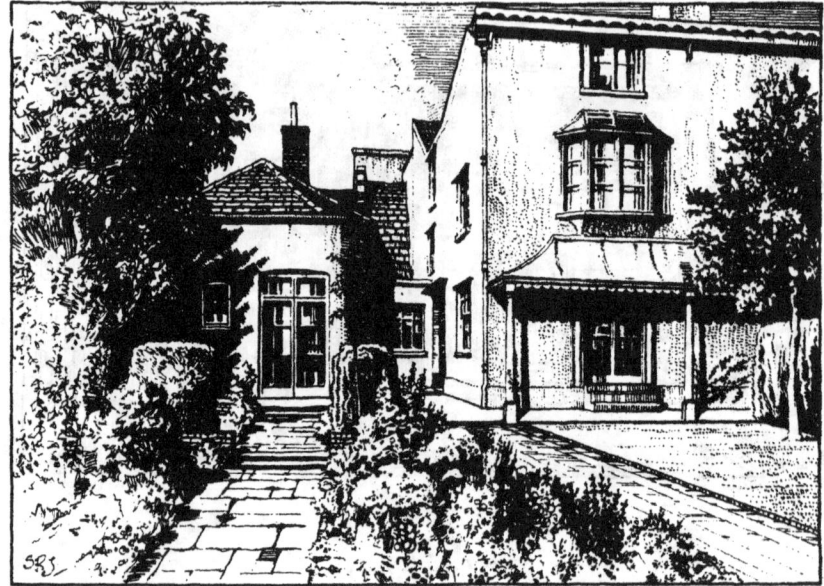

Everyone who really wants to draw houses, and means to succeed, is bound to reap the reward through trying. The actual production of drawings ever brings pleasure and satisfaction, and the creation of things personal and original is stimulating. None of us need mind disappointments, for new hands and old hands all make mistakes. By keeping on trying, it is soon realized that each new attempt teaches fresh lessons, that practice makes perfect. I have known people who were surprised at their gains in skill, after first thinking they would never be able to draw their own homes. There are great advantages, too, about drawing houses. They are near at hand. Everybody lives in one, making it possible at any time to decide just when and where to make a start.

By drawing houses, whether new or old, our own, or other people's, we also realize the differences in them ; can tell why some will look well on the paper, and why others may not. We get to know much of the beauty in form and colour, discover a great deal about walls, roofs, doorways, windows, and chimneys, and learn to understand the meaning of the craftsmanship that contributes to all good building. This knowledge helps with our own homes, serves to keep the standards of them high ; it fosters the desire for the best if, and when, a new home is thought of. When all the world thinks that way, ugly houses cannot be built, for people will not live in them. And everybody ought to live in a convenient house that is, in addition, a beautiful home. It makes such a difference to life.

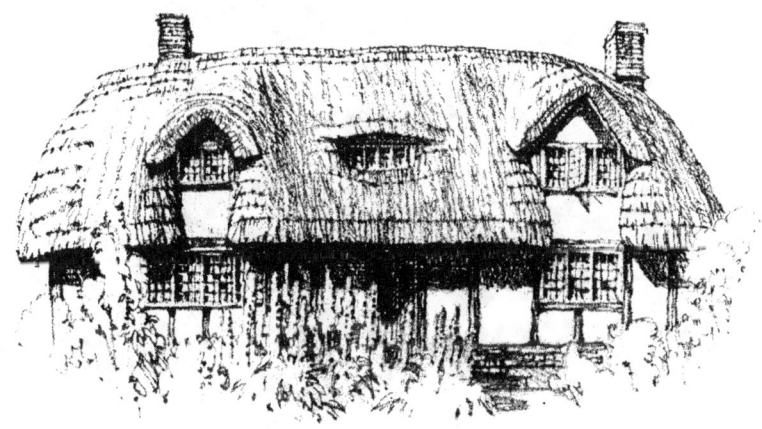

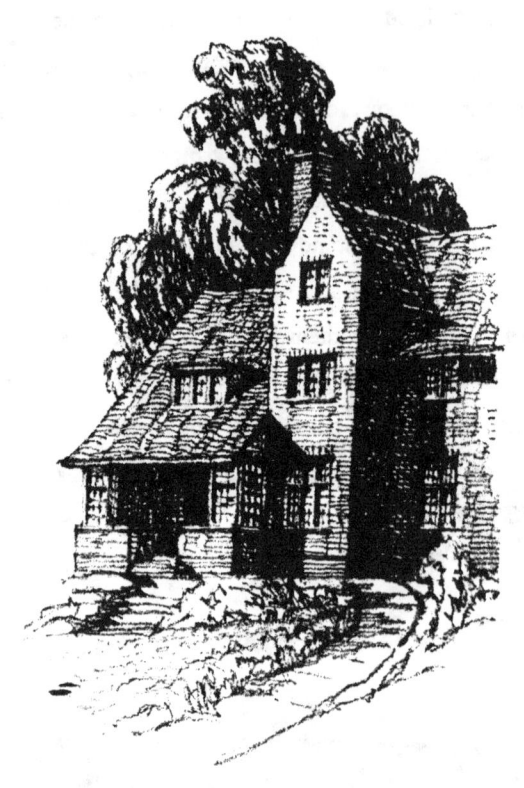

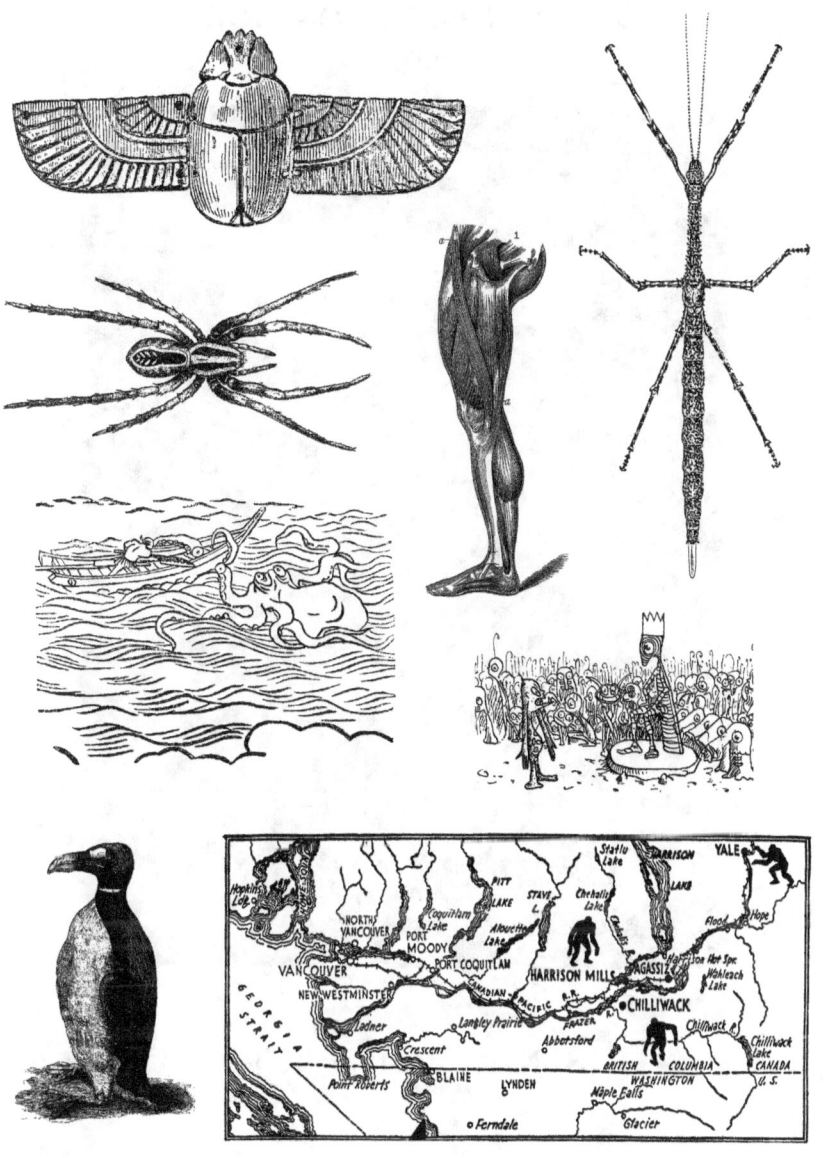

Coachwhip Publications

CoachwhipBooks.com

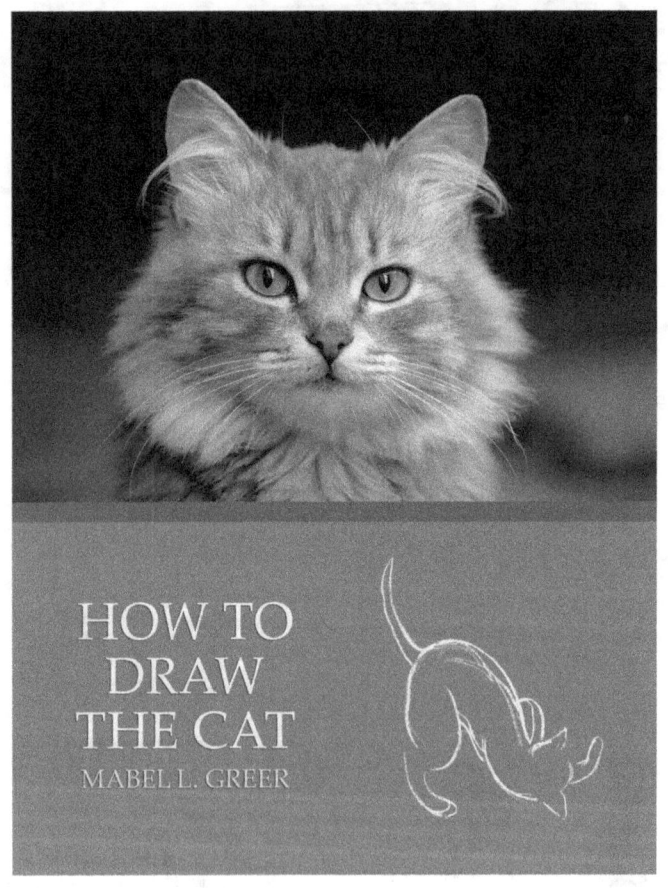

ISBN 978-1-61646-189-8

Coachwhip Publications

CoachwhipBooks.com

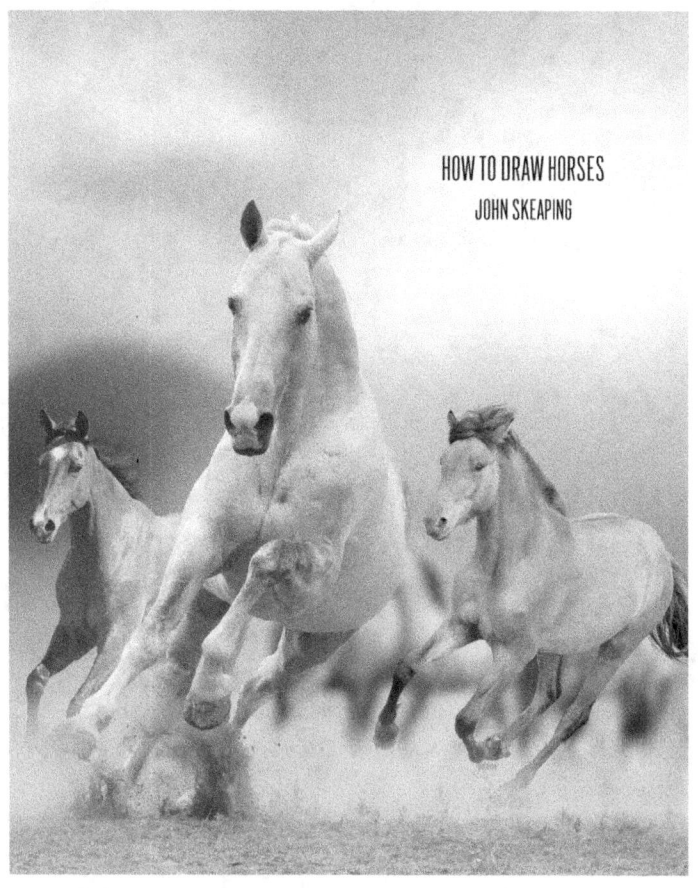

HOW TO DRAW HORSES
JOHN SKEAPING

ISBN 978-1-61646-190-4

COACHWHIP PUBLICATIONS

COACHWHIPBOOKS.COM

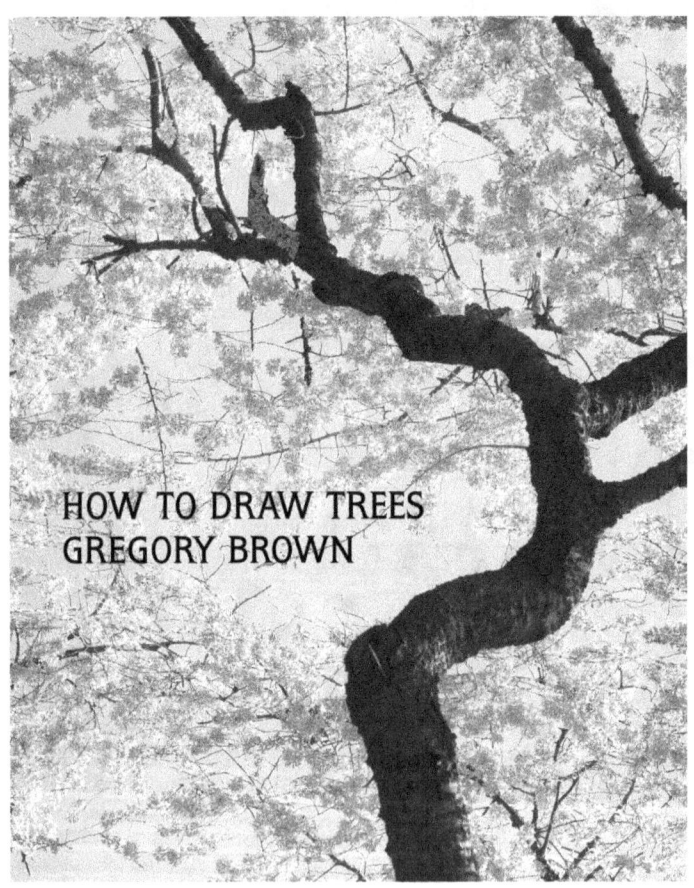

HOW TO DRAW TREES
GREGORY BROWN

ISBN 978-1-61646-194-2

COACHWHIP PUBLICATIONS

COACHWHIPBOOKS.COM

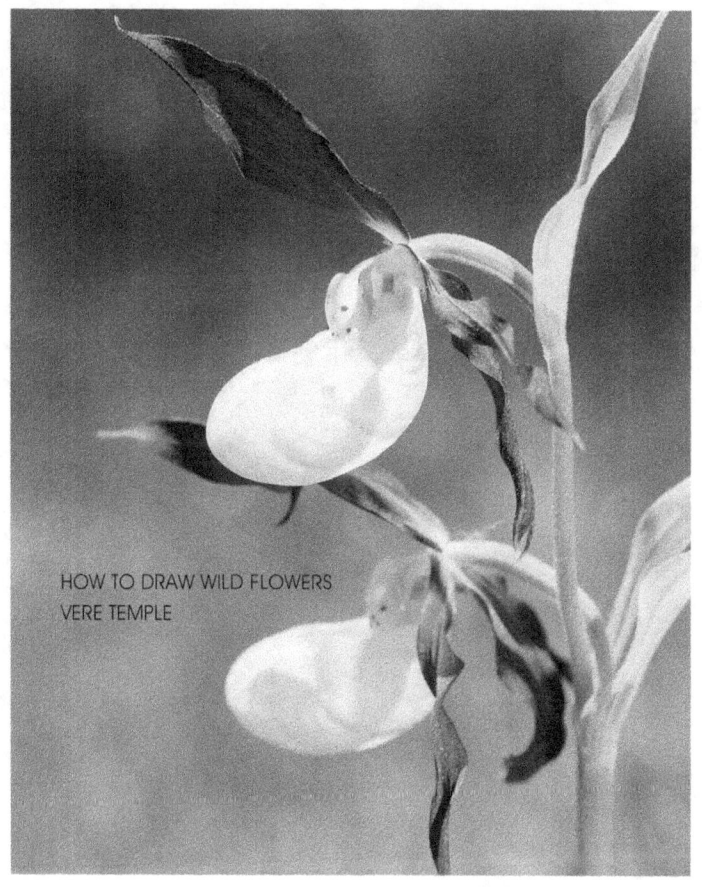

HOW TO DRAW WILD FLOWERS
VERE TEMPLE

ISBN 978-1-61646-196-6

www.ingramcontent.com/pod-product-compliance
Lightning Source LLC
Chambersburg PA
CBHW081304170526
45165CB00011B/3402